Contents

Introduction

Background

The Office of the Comptroller of the Currency's (OCC) *Comptroller's Handbook* booklet, "Student Lending," is prepared for use by OCC examiners in connection with their examination and supervision of national banks and federal savings associations (collectively, banks). Each bank is different and may present specific issues. Accordingly, examiners should apply the information in this booklet consistent with each bank's individual circumstances. When it is necessary to distinguish between them, national banks and federal savings associations (FSA) are referred to separately.

This booklet focuses on private student lending. Information regarding federal student loans is included as industry background, for historical context, and to highlight differences between federal student loans and private student loans. This booklet discusses how banks may legally and prudently engage in private student lending and the risks inherent in such lending; provides information on unique aspects of private student loans and industry practices; and includes private student lending product information, the processes involved in lending and risk management functions, and regulatory expectations for safe and sound operations.

The booklet provides additional notes on guaranteed rehabilitated student loans, a pool of loans that a small number of OCC-regulated community and midsize banks have shown interest in and have added to their balance sheets.

Regulatory Considerations

The regulatory considerations for national banks and FSAs are discussed throughout this booklet. One notable consideration for FSAs, which does not apply to national banks, is section 5(c)(1)(U) of the Home Owners' Loan Act.[1] This statute allows FSAs to invest in, sell, or otherwise deal in loans and other investments made for the payment of educational expenses without any limit on the aggregate amount of such loans.

General Information

The student lending market began with the passage of the Higher Education Act of 1965 (HEA).[2] This federal law governs the administration of federal student aid programs that provide financial assistance to students in postsecondary and higher education. Title IV of the HEA, which covers "financial assistance for students," authorized the federal guaranteed student loan program. The law was intended to strengthen the educational resources of colleges and universities and to provide financial assistance for students in postsecondary and

---

[1] Refer to 12 USC 1464(c)(1)(U), "Federal Savings Associations: Loans or Investments Without Percentage of Assets Limitation: Educational Loans," and generally 12 USC 1461 et seq.

[2] Refer to Public Law 89-329, 79 Stat 1219 (1965) (codified as 20 USC 1000 et seq.).

higher education. Among other things, the HEA increased federal money given to universities and awarded low-interest loans to students. Over the years, Congress has periodically reauthorized the HEA and has amended programs, changed the language and policies of existing programs, and established the statutory pricing of federal student loans.

The following are some of the federal student loan programs that have been available to students and their parents to finance postsecondary education:

- **William D. Ford Federal Direct Loan Program (Direct Loan Program):**[3] These loans are made by the U.S. Department of Education rather than by private financial institutions. The Direct Loan Program comprises four types of loans: Direct Subsidized Stafford Loans,[4] Direct Unsubsidized Stafford Loans, Direct Parental Loans for Undergraduate Students (Direct PLUS Loans), and Direct Consolidation Loans (consolidation loans). These loans are direct obligations of the Education Department, are not underwritten, and have not been securitized.
- **Federal Perkins Loan Program:**[5] These are low-interest, long-term loans intended for undergraduate, graduate, and professional students with exceptional financial need. The federal government subsidizes Perkins loans, meaning interest does not accrue until the loan enters repayment. In the Federal Perkins Loan Program, federal funds are delivered to the educational institution, which then becomes the lender. The borrower makes payments to the educational institution or to the educational institution's loan servicer.
- **Federal Family Education Loan Program (FFELP):**[6] The passage of the Health Care and Education Reconciliation Act of 2010 (HCERA) ended FFELP. While FFELP no longer exists, banks that used to participate in FFELP may still be managing a runoff[7] portfolio. These were loans funded by private banks and guaranteed by the federal government through the Education Department. Through FFELP, the federal government used to provide subsidies to private banks to offer federally insured loans that included subsidized and unsubsidized Stafford Loans, Direct PLUS Loans, and consolidation loans.

The federal government's role in financing postsecondary and higher education has grown significantly, and the government has now become the dominant source of financing.

---

[3] This is a student loan program authorized by Title IV, part C, of the HEA (20 USC 1087a et seq.). Refer to 34 CFR 685.100.

[4] The interest on a Direct Subsidized Stafford Loan is paid for by the federal government while the student is in school and during certain periods of deferment.

[5] This is a student loan program authorized by the HEA, Title IV, part D (20 USC 1087aa et seq.). Refer to 34 CFR 673, "General Provisions for the Federal Perkins Loan Program, Federal Work-Study Program, and Federal Supplemental Educational Opportunity Grant Program." Also refer to 34 CFR 674, "Federal Perkins Loan Program."

[6] This is a student loan program formerly authorized by Title IV, part B, of the HEA (20 USC 1071 et seq.). Refer to 34 CFR 682, "Federal Family Education Loan (FFEL) Program."

[7] The term "runoff" is defined as reduction of a loan portfolio as loans are paid off at scheduled maturity dates while no new business is being booked.

Alternative loans or private student loans are loans offered through lending programs funded by private lending institutions. By offering private student loans, banks generally provide a supplement to the federal government in financing postsecondary and higher education, e.g., when the maximum federal student loan available to a student is less than the cost of attending a school.

Business Model

Private student loans are consumer loans offered to borrowers to fund undergraduate, graduate, and other forms of postsecondary education. Under Regulation Z (12 CFR 1026.46(b)(5)), a private education loan means an extension of credit that

- is not made, insured, or guaranteed under Title IV of the HEA (20 USC 1070 et seq.).
- is extended to a consumer expressly, in whole or in part, for postsecondary educational expenses, regardless of whether the loan is provided by the educational institution that the student attends.
- does not include open-end credit or any loan that is secured by real property or a dwelling.
- does not include an extension of credit in which the covered educational institution is the creditor if
  - the term of the extension of credit is 90 days or less; or
  - an interest rate will not be applied to the credit balance and the term of the extension of credit is one year or less, even if the credit is payable in more than four installments.

Before the financial crisis began in 2008 and before FFELP was discontinued, some lenders operated on an integrated business model that included both federal guaranteed and private student loans. Banks held legal title to FFELP loans and received claim payments from eligible guarantors if eligible borrowers defaulted. FFELP loans generated income for banks in the form of interest income, interest subsidy payments,[8] default reimbursement, and special allowance payments.[9] Interest subsidy payments were paid while the students were in school, during the grace period, and during certain periods of deferment. FFELP loans received a 97 percent to 100 percent guarantee of principal and accrued interest, with reimbursement contingent on following the Education Department's servicing guidelines and due diligence requirements.[10]

---

[8] Interest subsidy payments are in-school interest payments on certain subsidized student loans paid for by the Education Department.

[9] Special allowance payments were subsidies from the Education Department to FFELP lenders to ensure that lenders received a minimum rate of return. Special allowance payments acted as an incentive for lenders to make education loans by, in effect, making up the difference between the interest rate charged to a FFELP borrower and market interest rates.

[10] Refer to *Common Manual: Unified Student Loan Policy,* chapters 10 and 12. This resource is a cooperative effort of all the nation's guarantors that participate in FFELP.

The financial crisis altered the banking landscape dramatically, resulting in fewer bank participants in postsecondary education lending and changes in banks' strategies. Banks had to reassess the long-term risk and return aspects of the private student loan business and make conscious decisions regarding the level and extent of their involvement in postsecondary education lending. Several large banks either withdrew or scaled back their private student loan offerings. Community banks, too, have been affected, and in many cases found it difficult to compete with the product array and pricing offered by larger institutions and the federal government. There are very few banks still engaged in private student lending, and those banks generally keep their portfolio exposures to a minimum. Today, the overall size of the private student loan portfolio is considered small compared with the overall size of the federal student loan portfolio. A small number of community banks, however, found an emerging opportunity in the federal guaranteed rehabilitated student loan program.[11]

The disruption in the securitization market during the financial crisis forced banks to alter their strategies. Banks that were originating and selling both FFELP and private student loans as asset-backed securities in the secondary market were forced to keep them in bank portfolios.

Most significantly, when the HCERA eliminated FFELP, the role of banks in federal student lending was discontinued for new loans. On July 1, 2010, the Direct Loan Program replaced FFELP[12] and it has been the only source of new federal student loans since then. These loans are obtained through the educational institution's financial aid office with funds provided by the Education Department. The terms and features of the federal student loans under the Direct Loan Program are similar to the terms and features of the federal student loans previously available through FFELP.

Although FFELP has been eliminated, banks continue to own and service loans made under FFELP. Because of their long repayment terms (120 to 360 months), runoff FFELP loans remain in the banks' portfolios. It is not unusual for examiners to find banks with both private student loan and federal guaranteed student loan exposures on their balance sheets.

Private student loans supplement federal student loans when federal student loans and other financial aid are not sufficient to cover the entire cost of education. Borrowers attending high-cost institutions or pursuing advanced degrees may turn to private student loan programs for additional financing. Banks should strongly encourage their borrowers to exhaust scholarships, grants, other financial aid, and federal student loans before applying for private student loans.

Student loan growth is not normally tied to the same factors that drive consumer lending, such as economic cyclicality, housing prices, and disposable income. In fact, student lending

---

[11] Refer to the "Rehabilitated Federal Student Loans" section of this booklet for a discussion of the Federal Rehabilitation Student Loan Program.

[12] FFELP's elimination only prohibited the making of new FFELP loans. If the first disbursement of a FFELP loan occurred before July 1, 2010, further disbursements of that loan could continue under FFELP.

exhibits some counter-cyclicality. A poor job market often encourages student borrowing because securing a college degree can improve job prospects. Some students may stay in school to avoid competing in a poor job market.

There is heightened public awareness and public policy attention centered on all participants in student lending. Banks should be mindful of the unique aspects of student lending, such as the significant time lag between loan advances and repayment, and the student borrower's lack of certainty in finding a stable, reliable primary source of repayment after graduation. Banks should pursue student lending in a measured and deliberate way. If managed and administered in an appropriate manner, student lending could benefit banks by providing them with a wider array of consumer products and a more diverse business model, and helping them reach new customers.

Private Student Loan Features

Most retail loan products are straightforward in terms of underwriting, loan structure, and account management. The use of funds is for a specific purpose, and the source of repayment is well-defined, well-structured, and typically verified as reliable at origination. Private student loans are less straightforward and require lenders to adapt loan structures and repayment terms to product characteristics.

Private student loans fund postsecondary education, are geared to the educational purpose of the loans and borrower needs, and require a substantial, long-term commitment. These loans lack collateral, and there is a significant time lag between loan advances and stable, reliable primary sources of repayment. This last factor is particularly important and often leads to differences in underwriting, loan repayment structures, and borrower assistance during repayment. Private student loans generally are not dischargeable in bankruptcy.[13]

Student loan repayment structures (federal and private) generally provide in-school deferment and post-school grace periods that help borrowers transition from in-school status to full-time employment. Student loans generally are the only consumer product with such a transition.

Banks that offer private student loans generally require borrower enrollment in degree-seeking programs. Private student loan features vary by target market and finance different education programs, including undergraduate, law, and business; medical, dental, and other health-related education; and general graduate studies, parent loans for students pursuing these programs, and loans to borrowers attending career schools and community colleges. Banks offer private student loans to specifically cover costs of medical boards and clinical exams, medical residency interview and relocation, internships, and costs associated with studying for a bar exam for law graduates. Some banks offer consolidation loans to simplify and streamline borrower repayment into a single payment and billing due date.

---

[13] Refer to 11 USC 523(a)(8), "Exceptions to Discharge." Private student loans generally are not dischargeable in bankruptcy if they are originated for borrowers attending schools eligible to participate in federal student loan programs. Private student loans extended to students in programs without access to federal funding (i.e., certain trade schools) may be dischargeable in bankruptcy.

Examiners should consider whether banks are appropriately setting the product requirements, term, pricing, and loan limits, and whether these features meet borrower needs and circumstances. Additionally, policies and procedures should provide adequate guidance to ensure that loans offered to borrowers are consistent with their needs, objectives, and financial conditions.

Federal Student Loans Versus Private Student Loans

Examiners should consider the unique aspects of student loans and understand that there are significant differences and relative similarities between federal student loan programs (FFELP and Direct Loan) and private student loans.

Differences

- **Loss guarantees:** FFELP loans received loss guarantees of 97 percent to 100 percent depending on origination dates. FFELP loans originated before October 1993 received a 100 percent guarantee; loans originated between October 1993 and June 2006 received a 98 percent guarantee; and loans originated on or after July 1, 2006, received a 97 percent guarantee. In contrast, private student loans do not carry any such federal government guarantee. To mitigate private student loan losses, some banks purchased loan loss insurance from third-party insurers. The disruption in the insurance market in 2008 ended this practice.
- **Application:** A borrower must complete and file the Free Application for Federal Student Aid (FAFSA) form with the educational institution's financial aid office to apply for a federal student loan. No FAFSA form is required to apply for a private student loan.
- **Pricing and loan amount:** Interest rates and loan borrowing limits on federal student loans are set by statute for all eligible borrowers under a particular loan program.[14] Private student loan interest rates and loan amounts are risk-based.
- **Criteria:** The borrower eligibility criteria for federal student loans allow most borrowers to qualify. Federal eligibility criteria rely on federal needs analysis methodology and do not, in most cases, employ credit checks, with the exception of PLUS loans.[15] Private student loans are underwritten based on a set of risk-based, lender-developed credit criteria that consider the borrower's credit history and ability to repay, and often require a cosigner(s).

---

[14] 20 USC 1087e(b)(8), "Terms and Conditions of Loans: Interest Rate Provisions for New Loans On or After July 1, 2013," establishes the current interest rates for direct loans. 20 USC 1077a, "Applicable Interest Rates," established maximum interest rates for federal guaranteed loans made under FFELP, including Direct PLUS Loans.

[15] Under 20 USC 1087kk et seq., the term "needs analysis" is defined as a standardized assessment of a student's or a student's family's ability to contribute toward educational expenses.

- **Default:** The Education Department defines a default on a federal student loan as occurring after 270 days of nonpayment.[16] A private student loan is in default after 120 days of nonpayment.[17]
- **Workout program:** Any workout program offered by banks to financially distressed private borrowers should follow existing banking guidance, and adhere to generally accepted accounting principles (GAAP) in determining if the loan constitutes a troubled debt restructuring (TDR). Federal student loan statutes do not have the same requirements.
- **Collection tools:**
  - A lawsuit is the main tool available to banks to pursue collection of defaulted private student loans. In contrast, defaulted federal student loans can be pursued using additional tools outside of court, including seizure of tax refunds, garnishment of wages without a court order, denial of other financial student aid and grants, taking a portion of Social Security benefits received, and revocation of professional or vocational licenses.
  - Depending on the state, banks may have to consider the applicable statute of limitations to enforce private student loan court judgments. Some states allow banks to continuously renew the judgments to prevent them from being subjected to statute of limitations. In comparison, there are no statutes of limitations for collection on federal student loans.[18]

Similarities

- **Academic year basis:** Both federal and private student loan programs generally grant or separately approve loans for each academic year.[19]
- **In-school deferment and grace period:** Both federal and private student loan programs generally allow the deferment of payments while borrowers are attending school at least

---

[16] For federal student loans, default is the failure of a borrower (or endorser or co-maker, if any) to make installment payments when due, if this failure persists for the most recent period of 270 days (for a loan repayable in monthly installments) or the most recent 330-day period (for a loan repayable in less frequent installments). Refer to *Common Manual: Unified Student Loan Policy,* "Appendix G: Glossary."

[17] Refer to OCC Bulletin 2000-20, "Uniform Retail Credit Classification and Account Management Policy: Policy Implementation."

[18] Section 484A(a) of the HEA provides that no statute of limitations bars enforcement action to collect federal student loans, including collection by offset, lawsuit, or enforcement on student loan judgments. 20 USC 1091a(a), "Statute of Limitations, and State Court Judgments," states that state law that would otherwise limit these actions is superseded by federal law and cannot bar collection action.

[19] The Education Department uses the academic year for determining a borrower's Title IV aid eligibility. The term "academic year" is defined as a period during which an undergraduate, full-time student is expected to complete either of the following: (1) at least 30 weeks of instructional time and 24 semester or trimester hours, or 36 quarter hours in an educational program that measures program length in credit hours, or (2) at least 26 weeks of instructional time and 900 clock hours in an educational program that measures program length in clock hours. Refer to *Common Manual: Unified Student Loan Policy,* "Appendix G: Glossary."

- half time. Both types of programs generally provide for a six-month grace period after graduation or separation from school before repayment begins.
- **Bankruptcy:** Both private and federal student loans generally are not dischargeable in bankruptcy unless borrowers can establish that repaying the loans would cause "undue hardship."[20]

Risks Associated With Private Student Lending

From a supervisory perspective, risk is the potential that events will have an adverse effect on a bank's current or projected financial condition[21] and resilience.[22] The OCC has defined eight categories of risk for bank supervision purposes: credit, interest rate, liquidity, price, operational, compliance, strategic, and reputation. These categories are not mutually exclusive. Any product or service may expose a bank to multiple risks. Risks also may be interdependent and may be positively or negatively correlated. Examiners should be aware of this interdependence and assess the effect in a consistent and inclusive manner. Examiners also should be alert to concentrations that can significantly elevate risk. Concentrations can accumulate within and across products, business lines, geographic areas, countries, and legal entities. Refer to the "Bank Supervision Process" booklet of the *Comptroller's Handbook* for an expanded discussion of banking risks and their definitions.

The risks associated with private student lending are credit, operational, compliance, liquidity, strategic, reputation, and interest rate.

Credit Risk

Credit risk is the most significant risk in private student lending. Private student loans are atypical of consumer loans because banks generally rely on the student borrower's *prospective* ability to repay. Private student loans finance a postsecondary education that often requires a considerable loan amount and a long-term bank commitment. These loans lack collateral, and there usually is a significant time lag between loan advances and the start of repayment. Borrowers are expected to graduate and generate a stable, reliable primary source of repayment, but whether they will actually do so is uncertain. Banks take on the credit risk based on reasonable assumptions of the borrower's and cosigner's ability to repay. Banks engaged in private student lending not only rely on traditional consumer lending criteria but also consider school eligibility criteria, such as program completion, graduation

---

[20] Refer to 11 USC 523(a)(8), "Exceptions to Discharge."

[21] Financial condition includes impacts from diminished capital and liquidity. Capital in this context includes potential impacts from losses, reduced earnings, and market value of equity.

[22] Resilience recognizes the bank's ability to withstand periods of stress.

rates, and the cost of attendance.[23] Without considering school eligibility factors, banks could be exposed to higher credit risk.

Consumer attitudes toward debt, affordability of higher education, underwriting standards, federal education policy, government public interests, and risk layering all can affect credit risk in private student loans. The effects of these factors are more pronounced for banks that lend to higher-risk borrowers with limited credit history and no direct source of repayment. In addition, private student loans can have elevated credit risk due to their variable rate feature and extended repayment terms. An unreasonable repayment period without consideration of the loan size may contribute to credit risk. Borrowers and cosigners who use deferment to delay loan repayment could pose increased credit risk to the bank. While in deferment, the loan amount continues to increase because of capitalized interest and may mean higher cost to borrowers.

Concentration risk is related to and affects credit risk. Concentration risk in private student lending can result from originating a large volume of loans to a specific class of borrowers, product type, and educational institution, or to borrowers affected by common economic events. Credit risk exists throughout the lending cycles of private student loans. These cycles include acquisition, initial underwriting, account management, and collection. Similar to other consumer loans, private student lending involves grouping homogeneous loans when credit risk is evaluated and managed on a segment or pooled basis.

Credit risk can be reduced in several ways. Banks should have a rigorous process of assessing their risk appetite, establishing product concentration limits measured as a percentage of capital, and charting forward-looking business strategies. Banks can control their credit risks by having strong credit risk management processes to guard against the unexpected and to measure, monitor, and control risks. Banks should have clearly documented and updated policies and procedures, underwriting standards, effective collection programs, and good management information systems (MIS).

Examiners assess credit risk in private student lending by evaluating portfolio performance, profitability, borrower profiles, products, and markets. Examiners should consider changes in underwriting standards, account acquisition channels, the credit score system used by the bank, and its marketing strategy.

Operational Risk

Similar to other retail loan products, student loan credit operations are primarily process-based and rely extensively on technology and automation along with ongoing innovation. For example, most banks have an application processing system (auto-decision system) that is

---

[23] The cost of attendance (COA) is an estimate of the student's educational expenses for the period of enrollment. The COA estimate should include tuition and fees, room and board, books and supplies, transportation, and personal expenses. COA is used solely for determining financial aid. The COA should include only those costs already incurred, or expected to be incurred, by the student over the course of the loan period. COA may not include outstanding charges or fees from a previous period of enrollment.

programmed to streamline the student loan decision process. The process systematically approves applicants who meet preapproved requirements. Banks employ credit scoring[24] technology. Because the operations tend to be so highly automated, banks should manage the processes prudently and maintain the systems and controls necessary to effectively identify, measure, monitor, and control operational risk.

Almost all banks engaged in student lending use third parties to perform various operational functions, such as loan acquisition and origination, servicing, and collections. Increased due diligence is required in these situations to minimize operational risk. Outsourcing specific activities may provide enhanced profitability; the risk, however, remains with the banks. OCC Bulletin 2013-29, "Third-Party Relationships: Risk Management Guidance," sets forth supervisory expectations in this area for banks.

Fraud is another operational risk present in private student lending. Banks should guard against private student loan fraud by verifying that funds are used to pay borrowers' tuition and other education expenses. Operating through the school channel versus a direct-to-consumer channel allows for such verification.

Examiners assess operational risk by evaluating the adequacy of private student loan application, processing, loan servicing, and collections systems and controls. Examiners should consider the volume of accounts managed, the capabilities of systems and technologies in relation to current and prospective volume, contingency preparedness, and exposures throughout the servicing system.

Compliance Risk

A significant number of consumer-related laws and regulations affect private student lending and make this type of lending vulnerable to compliance risk. The origination and collection of private student loans are subject to federal and state consumer protection laws and regulations. Banks' failure to comply with such laws and regulations could result in the assessment of fees, penalties, and adverse ratings. The following is a list of some of the consumer-related laws and regulations[25] applicable to private student lending:

- The Truth in Lending Act of 1968 (TILA), as implemented by Regulation Z (12 CFR 1026), and amended by the Higher Education Opportunity Act of 2008, which

---

[24] Credit scorecards provide an objective, numerical measure of a borrower's creditworthiness based on statistical models that evaluate performance and other factors. Credit scorecards, also referred to as models, are risk-ranking tools that attempt to differentiate between accounts that will exhibit "good" behavior and those that will not. (The definition of "bad" accounts varies but typically involves some level of delinquency, usually 60+ or 90+ days past due.) The scores generated indicate the relative level of risk in either ascending or descending order, depending on the convention used by the model developer. Credit scoring also is used to control risk in acquisition and underwriting, account management, and collection processes.

[25] Other *Comptroller's Handbook* booklets in the *Consumer Compliance* series address these laws and regulations more fully. For each of these laws and regulations, refer to the relevant booklet, which includes updated information and complete examination procedures.

added disclosure, timing, and other requirements for lenders making private education loans.[26] Regulation Z contains rules on disclosures, limitations on changes in terms after approval, the right to cancel the loan, and limitations on co-branding[27] in the marketing of private education loans (12 CFR 1026.46 to 12 CFR 1026.48).

- The Electronic Fund Transfer Act of 1978 (EFTA), as implemented by Regulation E (12 CFR 1005), which governs electronic fund transfers, such as telephone bill payments from borrowers and remote banking programs.[28]
- The Fair Debt Collection Practices Act of 1977 (FDCPA) and as subsequently amended, which is designed to eliminate certain abusive, deceptive, and unfair debt collection practices by debt collectors (generally those who regularly collect, or attempt to collect, consumer debts for another person or institution, or use a name other than their own when collecting their consumer debts).[29]
- The Fair Credit Reporting Act of 1970 (FCRA), as implemented by Regulation V (12 CFR 1022), which, among other requirements, imposes duties on furnishers of information to consumer reporting agencies.[30]
- The Equal Credit Opportunity Act of 1974 (ECOA), as implemented by Regulation B (12 CFR 1002), which prohibits discrimination in any aspect of a credit transaction and requires banks to provide adverse action notices to consumers.[31]
- The Gramm–Leach–Bliley Act of 1999 (GLBA), as implemented by Regulation P (12 CFR 1016), which requires banks to provide privacy notices and limit information sharing in specific ways.[32]
- Section 5 of the Federal Trade Commission Act and sections 1031 and 1036 of the Dodd–Frank Wall Street and Consumer Protection Act of 2010, which together prohibit unfair, deceptive, or abusive acts or practices in banks' interactions with consumers.[33]
- The Servicemembers Civil Relief Act of 2003 (SCRA), which, among other relief provisions for servicemembers, requires creditors to reduce the interest rate on debt

---

[26] Refer to 15 USC 1638(e), "Transactions Other Than Under an Open End Credit Plan: Terms and Disclosure With Respect to Private Education Loans." Also refer to 15 USC 1650, "Preventing Unfair and Deceptive Private Educational Lending Practices and Eliminating Conflicts of Interest." TILA appears at 15 USC 1601 et seq.

[27] Refer to 12 CFR 1026.48, "Limitations on Private Student Loans."

[28] Refer to 15 USC 1693 et seq.

[29] Refer to 15 USC 1692 et seq.

[30] Refer to 15 USC 1681 et seq.

[31] Refer to 15 USC 1691 et seq.

[32] Refer to 15 USC 6801 et seq.

[33] Section 5 of the Federal Trade Commission Act is codified at 15 USC 45, and sections 1031 and 1036 of Dodd–Frank are codified at 12 USC 5531 and 5536, respectively.

incurred before entry into military service to no more than 6 percent upon receipt of a written request and a copy of military orders.[34]

- The Military Lending Act of 2006 (MLA), which applies to all student loans not excluded from TILA. The rule expands specific protections provided to servicemembers and their families under the MLA and addresses a wider range of credit products than the U.S. Department of Defense's previous regulation.[35]

Bank management should assess whether staff and third parties involved in marketing, loan processing, servicing, and collections activity comply fully with these laws and regulations. Equally important, examiners should be familiar with applicable laws and regulations that affect private student lending.

Liquidity Risk

Banks engaged in private student lending generally fund their portfolios either through asset-backed securitization or by leveraging the banks' deposit base, or a combination of the two. Banks are exposed to liquidity risk when student loans are not in active repayment. Most private student loan programs allow students who are in school or in grace, deferment, or forbearance periods to defer payment of principal or interest or both. These loans not in active repayment status do not generate cash flow. The time lag for loans in deferment and forbearance presents additional liquidity risk to banks in the form of increased durations of loans and possible increased default frequency.

For banks with off-balance-sheet private student loan exposures, interest and principal on bonds backed by such collateral may still be due during periods of reduced cash flow. To avoid shortfalls in available funds to make such payments, banks often include capitalized interest accounts to cover the amount of reduced cash flow expected on the specific portfolio.

Liquidity risk is present if banks securitize their private student loan portfolios. Underwriting standards and administrative policies and procedures may not meet market requirements or expectations. Such an event may increase costs or limit access to funding markets in the future. Portfolio composition and portfolio volatility affect the salability of portfolios to investors and for securitization. Examiners should refer to the "Asset Securitization" booklet of the *Comptroller's Handbook* for more information on securitization and on how to examine these activities.

Strategic Risk

Banks offering private student loans should understand and evaluate competition, market conditions, borrower behavior, and economic, regulatory, and environmental factors that affect the industry. When making any changes to strategic direction, such as offering new

---

[34] Refer to 50 USC 3901 et seq.

[35] Refer to 32 CFR 232, "Limitations on Terms of Consumer Credit Extended to Service Members and Dependents."

student loan products, altering pricing strategies, expanding product features, or encouraging growth, banks should consider relevant factors. Banks' decision to enter, exit, or otherwise change their participation in the market should have a sound basis rooted in thorough evaluation of all available information and due diligence.[36] Banks should realistically assess the risk involved in such decisions and evaluate whether these decisions are consistent with their management expertise, operating capacity, and resources, and align with their risk appetite and capital adequacy. The failure to properly assess these factors may expose banks to unnecessary and unanticipated strategic risk and financial loss.

Reputation Risk

Customer dissatisfaction due to operational breakdowns, general weaknesses in any aspect of the private student lending program, and inadequate policies and procedures can harm banks' reputation. Reputation risk can escalate if borrowers perceive that lending practices are unfair, deceptive, abusive, or predatory. Delegation of bank functions to third parties heightens reputation risk.

Technological and news media developments have made reputation risk more consequential than ever before for banks engaged in private student lending. Poor servicing of existing accounts or non-resolution of borrower issues can generate immediate headlines and negative publicity for banks. The 2008 financial crisis brought attention to the large amount of overall student debt (both federal and private). For many higher education stakeholders, it has been difficult to differentiate between bank and nonbank private student loan lenders. During the economic downturn, high unemployment along with increased student loan default (federal and private) exposed banks to negative headlines concerning private student loans. Private student loan portfolios may be small in scale and not material to the banks' overall business, but the reputation risk could be significant.

Appropriate systems and controls to identify, measure, monitor, and control reputation risk are critical to a bank's risk management.

Interest Rate Risk

Most private student loans have a variable rate feature that is sensitive to yield curve risk. Any shifts in the yield curve or flattening of the yield curve can have an adverse impact on the portfolio. Deferring payments while borrowers are in school at least half time is a common practice in private student lending. This unique characteristic of private student lending could make banks vulnerable to additional interest rate risk because of timing of cash flows and changes in both cash flow and earnings spread.

---

[36] Refer to OCC Bulletin 2004-20, "Risk Management of New, Expanded, or Modified Bank Products and Services: Risk Management Process." For FSAs, refer to OTS *Examination Handbook*, section 760.

Risk Management and Control Systems

Each bank should identify, measure, monitor, and control risk by implementing an effective risk management system appropriate for the size and complexity of its operations. When examiners assess the effectiveness of a bank's risk management system, they consider the bank's policies, processes, personnel, and control systems. Refer to the "Bank Supervision Process" booklet of the *Comptroller's Handbook* for an expanded discussion of risk management.

Marketing and Account Acquisition

Private student loan originations may rely on multiple marketing channels. These channels may include bank branches, direct mail, school referral, and online or Internet sourcing.

For the school referral channel, banks may employ sales forces that establish relationships with school financial aid offices as preferred lenders.[37] Banks target students at schools with applications generally submitted online. Banks use direct-to-consumer marketing and online channels to target borrowers and reach broader footprints. The most common method of application is through secure websites operated directly by banks or third parties. Banks use direct mail and sales staff focused on targeted schools.

Before the financial crisis, contractual relationships existed between banks and guaranty agencies that originated (underwrote), guaranteed, disbursed, and serviced private student loans on behalf of banks. Very few of these relationships survived the financial crisis.

Whatever channels banks employ to originate private student loans, banks should have the systems to monitor the performance of those channels and control any risks. Failure to implement strong control environments can lead to such problems as fraud, compliance issues, or a host of situations with unexpected consequences.

Banks that originate private student loans are bound by TILA requirements. The general rules applicable to the special disclosure requirements for private education loans are detailed in

---

[37] The Higher Education Opportunity Act defines a "preferred lender arrangement" as an arrangement or agreement between a creditor and a school under which the creditor provides loans to the school's students or their families, and the school recommends, promotes, or endorses the creditor's loans. The term "preferred lender arrangement" is defined in 20 USC 1019(8), "Preferred Lender Arrangement." 15 USC 1650(a)(5), "Preventing Unfair and Deceptive Private Educational Lending Practices and Eliminating Conflicts of Interest," contains a cross-reference to 20 USC 1019(8). The term is also discussed in 20 USC 1019a, "Responsibilities of Covered Institutions, Institution-Affiliated Organizations, and Lenders"; 20 USC 1019b, "Loan Information to Be Disclosed and Model Disclosure Form for Covered Institutions, Institution-Affiliated Organizations, and Lenders Participating in Preferred Lender Arrangements"; 20 USC 1094, "Program Participation Agreements"; and 15 USC 1638, "Transactions Other Than Under an Open End Credit Plan."

12 CFR 1026.46 and associated commentary. Banks must comply with Regulation Z requirements, which include the following:

- Disclosure requirements:[38]
  - Provide disclosures on or with applications or solicitations (12 CFR 1026.47(a)).
  - Provide disclosures on or with a notice of loan approval (12 CFR 1026.47(b)).
  - Provide disclosures before loan disbursement (12 CFR 1026.47(c)).
- Limitations on private education loans:
  - Prohibit co-branding in the marketing of private education loans (12 CFR 1026.48(a)), unless an arrangement is entered into by the creditor and school for its endorsement and the marketing includes the proper disclosures (12 CFR 1026.48(b)).
  - Provide 30 calendar days to accept the loan consistent with the borrower's right to accept loan terms (12 CFR 1026.48(c)).
  - Provide a three-day right to cancel after receipt of final disclosures (12 CFR 1026.48(d)).
  - Obtain self-certification from the borrower before loan consummation (12 CFR 1026.48(e)).
  - Require banks in preferred lender arrangements to provide certain information to the school for each type of private student loan that the bank offers (12 CFR 1026.48(f)).

Banks must comply with the rules and requirements in section 140 of TILA (15 USC 1650) that address the following:

- Prohibit any private educational lender from offering or providing any gift to a covered educational institution in exchange for any advantage related to the private educational lender's private education loan activities.
- Prohibit any private educational lender from directly or indirectly engaging in revenue sharing[39] with a covered educational institution.
- Prohibit co-branding, which means that a private educational lender may not use words, pictures, or symbols readily identified with the covered educational institution in the marketing of private education loans in any way that implies that the covered educational institution endorses the private education loans offered by the private educational lender.
- Prohibit any financial aid office employee, or other person who is employed in the financial aid office of a covered educational institution, or who otherwise has responsibilities with respect to private education loans or other financial aid of the institution, and who serves on an advisory board, commission, or group established by a private educational lender or group of such lenders, from receiving anything of value

---

[38] Model forms for these disclosures are available in Regulation Z's appendix H (pages H18–H23).

[39] The term "revenue sharing" is defined as "an arrangement between a covered educational institution and a private educational lender under which—(A) a private educational lender provides or issues private education loans with respect to students attending the covered educational institution; (B) the covered educational institution recommends to students or others the private educational lender or the private education loans of the private educational lender; and (C) the private educational lender pays a fee or provides other material benefits, including profit sharing, to the covered educational institution in connection with the private education loans provided to students attending the covered educational institution or a borrower acting on behalf of a student."

from the lender or group (other than reimbursement of reasonable expenses incurred as part of service on an advisory board, commission, or group).

- Prohibit prepayment or repayment fees or penalties.
- Require public disclosure of any contract or other agreement made between an institution of higher education and a card issuer or creditor for the purpose of marketing a credit card.

To manage risk, bank management should ensure that all private student lending origination and marketing activities have the appropriate oversight, provide necessary disclosures, and comply with applicable rules and regulations. When pursuing school preferred lender relationships, banks should make certain that all sales representatives follow appropriate codes of conduct and ethics that include compliance with the requirements of Regulation Z and section 140 of TILA.

Examiners should assess whether banks engaged in private student lending provide clear and conspicuous disclosures that contain the information required in 12 CFR 1026.47. This information includes topics such as applicable interest rates, fees, default and late payment costs, repayment terms, cost estimates, eligibility requirements, federal program alternatives to private student loans, the borrower's right to loan terms that remain generally unchanged for 30 days, and the prerequisite borrower self-certification requirement.[40] Banks must provide this information to borrowers and adequately address what borrowers need to know before obtaining private student loans. In addition, banks must comply with approval disclosure requirements as well as final disclosure requirements under section 12 CFR 1026.47.

Banks that use third parties to market, solicit, or originate private student loans should have third-party risk management frameworks that include

- due diligence in selecting third parties.
- written contracts that have been thoroughly vetted for duties, obligations, and responsibilities of all parties including compensation parameters.
- ongoing monitoring and quality assurance programs.

Banks should adhere to other regulatory expectations regarding risk management outlined in OCC Bulletin 2013-29, "Third-Party Relationships: Risk Management Guidance." Banks' risk management systems should reflect the complexity of third-party activities and the overall level of risk involved.

Private Student Lending Underwriting Standards

Banks' risk appetite, or the level of risk they are willing to take, is the basis of the banks' specific underwriting criteria. Higher education financing may be the only consumer product for which lenders generally consider cosigners' current ability to repay the loans rather than

---

[40] This list consists of the required preapproval disclosures in 12 CFR 1026.47(a), "Application or Solicitation Disclosures." The contents of the approval disclosures and the disbursement disclosures are different.

the borrowers' future income. Despite their unique purpose and nature, private student loans are unsecured retail credit products, and banks should adhere to safe and sound credit underwriting and documentation standards as stated in 12 CFR 30, appendix A, "Safety and Soundness Standards," that include the following:

Prudent credit underwriting practices that

- are commensurate with the types of loans banks will make and that consider the terms and conditions under which the loans will be made.
- consider the nature of the markets in which loans will be made.
- provide for consideration, before credit commitment, of borrowers' overall financial condition and resources, the financial responsibility of any guarantors, the nature and value of any underlying collateral, and borrowers' character and willingness to repay as agreed.
- establish a system of independent, ongoing credit review and appropriate communication to management and to the board of directors.
- take adequate account of capital planning consistent with strategic planning and associated concentration of credit risk.
- are appropriate to the banks' size and the nature and scope of the banks' activities.

Loan documentation practices that

- enable the banks to make informed lending decisions and to assess risk, as necessary, on an ongoing basis.
- identify the loans' purpose and sources of repayment and assess the borrowers' ability to repay the indebtedness in a timely manner.
- ensure that any claim against borrowers is legally enforceable.
- demonstrate appropriate administration and monitoring of loans.
- take account of the loans' size and complexity.

Private student loans vary significantly in terms of underwriting, pricing, maximum loan amounts, and repayment terms. Underwriting and product terms should appropriately recognize the risks of unsecured lending to a higher-risk borrower population (by virtue of unproven credit records). The ability of students to achieve gainful employment after graduation is one of the determinants of default frequency.

Private student loans should be carefully underwritten to minimize the occurrence of default or the need to provide repayment assistance. Banks should have adequate and sound credit policies and procedures that focus on the main criteria for decision-making and verification processes. The following are some of the underwriting factors and requirements that banks have used in private student lending:[41]

- Educational institution and education program
- Borrower and cosigner creditworthiness
- Maximum student debt per academic year and cost of attendance (COA)
- Marketing channel
- Credit bureau risk score
- Credit history
- Minimum gross income
- Income verification
- Loan features and structure
- Citizenship status and U.S. residency

Educational Institutions

Some private student lenders use factors relating to the educational institutions that borrowers attend for determining underwriting and pricing of private student loans.[42] Banks have considered

- educational institutions' financial history, accreditation, financial stability, and long-term viability.
- the average time and cost to complete degrees or programs.
- the average dropout, graduation, and completion rates.
- employment rates and average salaries for graduates and, if available, for dropouts.
- banks' own default rate experience regarding the educational institutions' borrowers who recently entered repayment.

When banks target borrowers enrolled at particular institutions or in specific education programs, comprehensive and effective due diligence is critical to understanding the level of risk assumed. Banks should update and review this information regularly, or at least annually, and perform the due diligence as long as the relationships with particular educational institutions continue.

Some banks consider lending only to borrowers attending educational institutions that pass the Education Department's eligibility criteria. School eligibility is defined by the Education Department as those institutions qualified to participate in Title IV of the HEA, and one of the required conditions for a school to qualify is to have an acceptable cohort default rate

---

[41] Banks using factors that may not be related to loan terms or borrower creditworthiness, such as the educational institution or citizenship status, should closely consider and monitor the fair lending implications of these factors. Refer to the "Educational Institutions" section of this booklet.

[42] Refer to GAO-10-86R, "Higher Education: Factors Lenders Consider in Making Lending Decisions for Private Education Loans," November 17, 2009.

(CDR) on federal student loans.[43] CDR consideration in private lending for school eligibility, underwriting, or pricing may have a disproportionate negative impact on minority students who disproportionately attend schools with higher CDRs.[44] Banks should carefully analyze the potential fair lending implications of using CDR and other non-individual factors and document the legitimate business need for their use.

Another criterion that banks generally consider is the type of educational institution. The Education Department defines three types of eligible institutions of higher education: public or private nonprofit institutions, proprietary institutions (private and for-profit), and public or private nonprofit postsecondary vocational institutions defined in 34 CFR 600.4, 34 CFR 600.5, 34 CFR 600.6, and 34 CFR 600.9. Banks that extend loans to borrowers who attend nontraditional education programs or alternative programs should take into consideration that certain trade schools or vocational institutions may not have access to federal funding under Title IV. Therefore, private student loans extended to finance attendance in these institutions may be dischargeable in bankruptcy.

To manage risk, banks should track loan performance and report on established concentration limits for each student loan program, geographic area, school type (graduate program, four- or two-year institution, or trade school), origination channel (e.g., school or online), and loan quality or risk grade.

Borrower Creditworthiness

Banks should have underwriting criteria designed to measure the borrowers' financial capacity, in terms of disposable income available for orderly debt repayment, and willingness to repay, typically based on past performance on financial obligations. Because there is no reliable method for considering future income or other future events in the underwriting process of private student loans, banks typically require cosigners on loans. This allows for additional borrower support if borrowers are unable to make loan payments after graduation or program completion.

A cosigner is any person who assumes personal liability, in any capacity, for the obligation of a borrower without receiving goods, services, or money in return for the obligation. The cosigner is equally and severally liable and is expected to make payments on the primary borrower's debt should that borrower default. Having a cosigner is a way for a private student loan borrower with a low income or poor or limited credit history to qualify for and obtain more favorable financing terms.

Most banks offer cosigners a release option after the initial 36 to 48 consecutive, on-time payments of principal and interest after repayment begins, subject to verification of the primary borrower's continuous ability to repay. Most banks offer cosigner release in the unfortunate event of the student borrower's death or total and permanent disability. Banks

---

[43] Refer to 34 CFR 668.206, "Consequences of Cohort Default Rates on Your Ability to Participate in Title IV, HEA Programs."

[44] Refer to Consumer Financial Protection Bureau (CFPB), Private Student Loans, page 80, August 29, 2012.

that offer the cosigner release option should keep track of this feature in the loan agreements and fulfill the terms.

A key component in underwriting student loan applications is the assessment of affordability of the loan and taking into account the borrowers' and cosigners' (if any) ability to meet all debt service requirements for existing and proposed loans. Banks may account for adequate margin in debt service requirements to protect against adverse changes in borrowers' and cosigners' (if any) circumstances.

When determining ability to repay, the bank's underwriting criteria rely heavily on the cosigner's income streams and assets while taking into account all of the cosigner's obligations. A credible analysis should conclude that the borrower and cosigner can meet all debt service requirements for existing and proposed loans using regularly amortizing payments.

In some private student loan programs, borrowers may be able to qualify on their own without the need for cosigners. To qualify, borrowers should have credit scores that meet the program minimums and may need to satisfy any employment, income, or asset requirements.

When evaluating borrowers' and cosigners' ability to repay, banks should consider all debt obligations, including monthly rent or mortgage, auto loans, other student loans (in repayment and deferment), alimony and child support, minimum credit card payments, and other debt payments.

The determination of borrowers' and cosigners' ability to repay should be based on reliable information, including documented and verified income. Some of the most common and acceptable documentation includes

- recent pay stubs.
- W-2 forms.
- evidence of payroll direct deposit.
- personal or business tax returns.
- signed 1099 forms.
- verification of employment through employer direct contact.
- divorce decree or other legal document to verify child support or alimony payments.
- other appropriate documentation, such as a social security award letter and investment statements.

Credit Bureau Risk Score

As a credit overlay, banks often use credit scores in loan underwriting and rely on credit bureau data to gauge credit history, payment experience, and performance. Credit scores project the probability of future payment performance based on past experience. For some banks, borrowers' credit scores serve as the key requirement in the decision to approve or decline applications in the underwriting process. Most banks, however, use credit scores for screening and subsequently perform additional review based on other credit criteria.

As with any other consumer loan product, banks that use credit scores in private student lending should control credit quality by setting appropriate cutoff scores based on acceptable default risk or loss rate. Bank management may change the cutoff credit score, and this change alters the risk profile of the originated loans. The cutoff credit score is one of the control mechanisms for volume (quantity) and profit (quality) in private student loans. As a basic principle, the higher the cutoff credit score, the lower the approval rate and fewer the delinquency problems. Decisions to change the cutoff credit score reflect a change of strategy, a change in quality of applicants, and a change in expected level of profitability. Bank management should ensure that credit scoring models are used appropriately and are functioning effectively. Bank management should

- thoroughly understand the credit scoring models.
- use credit scoring models for their intended purpose.
- validate or revalidate the credit scoring models' performance regularly.
- review tracking reports, including the performance of overrides.
- take appropriate action when the credit scoring models' performance deteriorates, including reviewing bank lending strategies to determine their effect on the credit scoring models; actively managing the credit scoring model cutoff strategies; or developing new credit scoring models.
- ensure the credit scoring models comply with fair lending regulations.

Credit scoring models used in student lending should be subject to sound model validation processes, including evaluation of conceptual soundness, ongoing monitoring, and outcomes analysis.

For a basic explanation of credit score models, refer to OCC Bulletin 1997-24, "Credit Scoring Models: Examiner Guidance," and OCC Bulletin 2011-12, "Supervisory Guidance on Model Risk Management."

Banks should have credit underwriting criteria that include measurements of borrowers' and cosigners' capacity to repay the loans (debt-to-income or payment-to-income), acceptable documentation, cutoff credit score and tolerance for overrides, and school eligibility requirements. Banks that have underwriting standards that are less stringent than industry and market standards should establish portfolio concentration limits on these lesser-qualified borrowers to minimize the banks' exposure to a manageable level.

Loan Feature and Structure

Banks offer a range of private student loan features and structures. Interest rates may be fixed or adjustable; repayment terms may be straight amortization or graduated; and repayment periods may be shorter (10 years or less) or longer (over 10 years). Banks generally consider these factors jointly in the qualification process and should develop a range of reasonable tolerances for each factor. Underwriting should be based on prudent and appropriate underwriting standards, taking into account borrowers' characteristics and private student loan attributes.

Banks that offer graduated repayment terms at origination should follow the prudent standards outlined in OCC Bulletin 2015-7, "Interagency Guidance on Private Student Loans With Graduated Repayment Terms at Origination." Borrowers and banks generally are best served by amortizing repayment of principal and interest over reasonable periods. When considering graduated repayment terms, banks should promote orderly repayment over the life of the loans. Banks should consider providing longer repayment periods (e.g., 20 years) for larger loans and shorter repayment periods for smaller loans.

Maximum Student Debt

Banks generally set private student loan amount limits according to the published cost of attendance at the borrowers' schools, with lifetime caps based on the students' programs of study. The schools set the overall loan limit for each student based on qualified education expenses up to the cost of attendance, less all other student aid received,[45] and any other loans already applied to the cost for the academic year.

Banks require school certification or verification of enrollment to ensure that students are borrowing responsibly and that the loan amounts requested do not exceed the borrowers' COA. School financial aid offices certify borrowers' need for loans and the amount that borrowers are eligible to borrow. School certification provides the following additional information: academic period, enrollment status and grade level, expected graduation date, and disbursement date. Federal law requires that before lenders may disburse private student loans, the lenders must obtain completed and signed self-certification forms[46] from borrowers.

Disbursement of funds may include certified checks jointly payable to the students and the schools, or electronic funds transfers of loan proceeds to student accounts at the eligible schools. Depending on the loan purpose, there is generally a cumulative limit[47] on total loans that banks grant and variation on loan terms (5, 10, 15, 20, or more years).

Pricing

Pricing is a key component of underwriting. Private student loans can have either a fixed interest rate or a variable interest rate. Fixed-rate loans are determined at the time of application approval and remain the same for the life of the loan. A variable rate is based on an index such as the London Interbank Offered Rate (LIBOR)[48] or prime lending rate plus a fixed margin rate determined by borrower and cosigner creditworthiness at the time of application. The variable index rate may change on a monthly or quarterly basis. Banks price

---

[45] Such aid includes grants, scholarships, fellowships, and financial awards.

[46] This information is included in the borrower's financial award letter from the school. The form is also available from the school's financial aid office.

[47] The cumulative limit includes both federal and private student loans.

[48] LIBOR is the average interest rate paid on deposits of U.S. dollars in the London market.

private student loans depending on the risk profiles of borrowers and cosigners. Loans that have cosigners generally are priced significantly lower than those without cosigners.

Banks should carefully balance pricing for risk and avoid errors that can threaten the portfolios and their performance. There are consequences if banks price below or above market. Any pricing above market could potentially create adverse selection, meaning only the least creditworthy private student loan borrowers apply. This happens because the lower-risk borrowers take advantage of less costly financing options available to them. The highest-risk borrowers apply for and accept retail credit at almost any rate.

Often, banks offer borrower benefits such as an interest rate reduction when repayment begins. The interest rate reduction generally ranges between 25 and 100 basis points and is provided if certain conditions are met, including the borrowers agreeing to automatic debit payments from personal checking or savings accounts, the borrowers making specified consecutive on-time payments, the borrowers graduating or completing programs, or the existence of qualifying bank relationships.

Examiners should assess whether the bank has well-defined underwriting criteria that establish prudent risk limits, including minimum credit scores, reasonable debt-to-income ratios, maximum loan amount and duration, and appropriate pricing.

Other Requirements

Except for continuing education loans, bank loans also require that borrowers be enrolled at least half time. In addition to credit qualification, private student loans are subject to completion of loan applications and consumer credit agreements, verification of application information, self-certification forms, and school certification.

Through the school channel, colleges or universities certify the loans. School certification means that the school validates that the student has been accepted and will attend the school through which he or she is applying for the loan. Using the school channel ensures that the borrower obtains only funds necessary for his or her education and that funds are distributed directly to the school, not the borrower. School verification of application includes checking the accuracy of information reported by the student on the FAFSA and may include requesting a copy of the student's tax returns and, if applicable, the student's parents' tax returns.

Banks should ensure that funds are being used to pay for borrowers' tuition and other education expenses. Most banks use the school channel instead of direct-to-consumer channel because the school channel is less susceptible to misuse of funds and fraud. Direct-to-consumer loans generally do not require school certification and can result in borrowers applying for funds in excess of the cost. Banks that use the direct-to-consumer channel release private student loan funds directly to borrowers and lose control over use of the funds.

Banks are expected to follow applicable laws and regulations when underwriting and originating private student loans, including the following:

- **TILA:** All disclosures are made in an accurate and timely manner, as required by TILA.
- **FCRA:** A credit bureau report is requested only if there is a permissible purpose to request it under the FCRA.
- **ECOA:** Loan programs must be administered in a nondiscriminatory manner (including marketing, underwriting, pricing, and servicing), and accurate and consistent adverse action treatment of all declined applications must be documented and followed as required by ECOA.
- **GLBA:** Privacy notices are provided, and information sharing is limited, as required by GLBA.
- **EFTA:** Electronic transfers of loan proceeds to consumers must comply with EFTA requirements.
- **Unfair or Deceptive Acts or Practices (UDAP) and Unfair, Deceptive, or Abusive Acts or Practices (UDAAP):** All elements of marketing, underwriting, and origination must comply with the prohibitions on unfair, deceptive, or abusive acts or practices contained in section 5 of the Federal Trade Commission Act of 1914 and Title X of Dodd–Frank.[49]

Underwriting Exceptions

Banks' private student lending underwriting policies and criteria should reflect the banks' stated risk appetites. Any underwriting exceptions could potentially change the risk profile of approved loans and the portfolios overall. The more discretion injected into the process, the higher the potential for exceptions. Policy exceptions generally are unavoidable because no underwriting policy is comprehensive enough to cover all possible situations. Banks should have the necessary MIS to identify and track exceptions.

Banks should establish limitations for each type of exception and monitor adherence to those limits. Reports should track all exceptions to significant underwriting policy, scoring, documentation, and school eligibility requirements. Bank management should ensure that the information is regularly analyzed to determine causes and impacts, and, when necessary, implement corrective action.

Examiners should assess whether banks' private student loan MIS have adequate detail to facilitate analysis of exceptions overall and by type to determine if exceptions significantly affect the portfolios' risk profiles. To make this determination, examiners should consider the exceptions' volume and trends and the ongoing performance of loans originated with exceptions. If the performance of loans originated with exceptions is weaker than that of loans conforming to underwriting criteria, bank management should require stricter adherence to underwriting policy. If performance is better, bank management should consider revising bank policy.

---

[49] Refer to OCC Advisory Letter 2002-3, "Guidance on Unfair or Deceptive Acts or Practices," which sets forth the OCC's guidance on unfair or deceptive acts or practices.

Exception and performance tracking should be sufficiently granular to enable the board and bank management to drill down into the sources of exceptions. By evaluating exceptions and subsequent performance by product, credit quality, school, channel, etc., bank management can target corrective action to the actual source of any problem.

Loan Servicing and Administration

Private student loan servicers are responsible for properly administering loans from origination through final payment. Banks or third parties perform student loan servicing. Using reliable third-party servicers can be an effective way to standardize procedures, facilitate growth, and minimize costs. Additionally, third-party servicers are more likely to have the scale, system infrastructure, and, in most cases, personnel experience to carry out any specialized student loan requirements (e.g., use of deferments and grace periods). Banks that use third-party servicers should ensure that loans are administered appropriately and comply with bank policies and procedures and applicable laws and regulations.[50] Banks should follow the supervisory guidelines regarding risk management outlined in OCC Bulletin 2013-29, "Third-Party Relationships: Risk Management Guidance." Banks' risk management systems should reflect the complexity of banks' third-party activities and the overall level of risk involved.

The following terminology is commonly associated with repayment of student loans:

- **In-school period:** The time during which the borrower is enrolled at least half time at an eligible school. The in-school period ends when the borrower graduates or leaves school, or when the borrower's enrollment drops below half time.[51]
- **In-school deferment:** A period during which no payment is required while the borrower is enrolled at a "qualifying" school, per the bank's definition, as no less than a half-time student.[52]
- **Repayment period:** The period during which payments of principal and interest are required. The repayment period typically follows any applicable in-school deferment or grace period.
- **Grace period:** A standard six-month period after graduation or withdrawal from school during which no payment is required. This grace period may be automatically granted to a borrower who leaves school or drops below half time before repayment begins.[53]
- **Extended grace period:** An additional, consecutive, one-time period during which no payment is required for up to six months after the initial grace period. An extended grace period typically is granted to the borrower who may be having difficulty finding

---

[50] These include the FDCPA (15 USC 1692 et seq.) and OCC Bulletin 2014-37, "Consumer Debt Sales: Risk Management Guidance."

[51] Refer to 34 CFR 685.207(b)(1).

[52] Refer to 34 CFR 685.204(b).

[53] Refer to 34 CFR 674.2(b).

employment before the repayment period starts. The extended grace period counts toward the maximum lifetime allowable payment forbearance of no more than 12 months.[54]

Repayment Terms

Banks generally offer various repayment options or repayment terms for student loans:

- **Immediate repayment:** This repayment option requires the borrower to begin making principal and interest payments, usually no more than 60 days after the final disbursement date of the loan.
- **Deferred principal and interest:** This option involves full deferment of principal and interest payments during school while capitalizing the accrued interest. Repayment begins six months after the earliest of (1) graduation, (2) the borrower ceasing to be enrolled in school, or (3) the borrower being enrolled less than half time. Banks generally have a limit on how long the deferment lasts, which is usually tied to the expected completion time period of the borrower's education program.
- **Fully amortizing repayment:** This option involves a periodic loan payment, part of which is principal and part of which is interest. If the borrower makes payments according to the loan's amortization schedule, the loan will be paid off by the end of its term. The borrower and the bank generally are best served by amortizing repayments of principal and interest over a reasonable time period.
- **Graduated repayment:** This repayment structure allows for lower monthly payments that gradually increase. Banks that offer this option at origination should follow safe and sound lending practices and regulatory principles outlined in OCC Bulletin 2015-7, "Interagency Guidance on Private Student Loans With Graduated Repayment Terms at Origination." Banks may offer borrowers graduated repayment terms in addition to fixed amortizing terms and provide flexibility to repay the debt sooner if borrowers' incomes increase more quickly than projected. When underwriting private student loans with graduated repayment, banks should consider aligning payment terms with the borrower's income. Banks should establish the time period during which graduated repayment terms will be offered, usually at the beginning of the repayment period.
- **Interest only:** Some banks may require some form of in-school repayment that includes full or nominal interest payment. Interest-only payments generally begin no more than 60 days after the final disbursement date.

Loan servicing includes all activities during the in-school, grace, and repayment periods. Loan servicing includes various activities, such as

- verifying the borrower's in-school status.
- transitioning to loan repayment.
- establishing repayment terms.
- applying payments.

---

[54] Refer to Chief National Bank Examiner Policy Guidance (CNBE) 2010-2 (REV), "Policy Interpretation: OCC Bulletin 2000-20—Application to Private Student Lending." This policy guidance previously was available only internally to OCC employees and is made public with this booklet.

- granting deferment and forbearance.
- reporting loan information to credit bureaus.
- responding to inquiries.

The loan servicer receives and processes updated enrollment information through various processes, including certification from applications, deferment forms, letters from a school official, the National Student Loan Data System—Student Status Confirmation Report (NSLDS-SSCR)[55] process, and direct communication from the school. When the loan servicer is notified that the borrower is no longer attending school or is not carrying the required credits, the borrower generally enters a grace period. The grace period is intended to provide the borrower with time to find employment and prepare to repay the loan. The borrower is generally allowed a six-month grace period before loan repayment begins.

During the grace period, the loan servicer is generally expected to establish a relationship with the borrower to help the borrower understand his or her repayment status and obligations, promote any self-service payment option offered by the bank (e.g., online), and obtain updated borrower contact information. The loan servicer should help educate and inform the borrower regarding the tools and options available to assist him or her in managing the student loan and options to receive bill correspondence electronically.

Management should ensure that loan servicers adhere to applicable federal laws and regulations, including the following:

- ECOA (Regulation B)
- EFTA (Regulation E)
- FCRA (Regulation V)
- FDCPA
- "Privacy of Consumer Financial Information" (Regulation P)
- USA PATRIOT Act
- TILA (Regulation Z)
- SCRA
- MLA

Because private student loans are unsecured debt and not federally guaranteed, loan servicers need to be highly proficient in ensuring that loans are properly originated and appropriately serviced. If banks use third-party servicers, these servicers generally indemnify banks and hold them harmless from liability for any deficiency in originating or servicing student loans. Indemnification is considered best practice when using third-party servicers. The strength of the indemnification is closely tied to the third party's financial condition, and importantly, indemnification provisions are not a substitute for proper risk-management practices.

---

[55] The NSLDS is a national database of information on Title IV aid, including FFELP loans. The NSLDS was developed to provide loan-level information on Title IV loans and to provide an integrated view of other Title IV programs. NSLDS overall goals are to improve the quality and accessibility of student aid data, reduce the burden of administering Title IV aid, and minimize abuse within the aid programs through accurate tracking of funds awarded to assist the postsecondary students for whom the programs were designed.

Examiners should expect banks to have a sound third-party program that includes periodic due diligence, review, and monitoring. Banks should conduct periodic on-site third-party servicer audits to assess whether the third parties are adhering to the banks' private student loan policies and procedures. Banks should have third-party metrics and appropriate MIS reports that include loan performance by third-party servicers. One of the key components of a third-party servicer program is a Statement on Standards for Attestation Engagements Number 16 review (SSAE 16). This annual review helps monitor third-party servicers' operational soundness and ability to comply with bank policies and procedures and applicable laws and regulations. Bank management should have appropriate processes and procedures when third-party servicers are given unacceptable or equivalent ratings during annual reviews.

Bank management should be mindful of student loan servicing deficiencies highlighted by the Consumer Financial Protection Bureau (CFPB)[56] in its annual ombudsman reports.[57]

Collections

In most banks, whether done in-house or through third parties, loan servicing is responsible for loan collections of private student loans. Loan servicers have specialized collections staff whose responsibilities may involve the collections of both private and federal guaranteed student loans. Whether private or federal, student loans are generally difficult to discharge in bankruptcy. There are time limits or statutes of limitations, however, on how long private student lenders can try to collect on the underlying debt. These time limits or statutes of limitation vary by state but are usually about three to six years.[58] If banks sue and obtain court judgments, the banks may have from five to as many as 20 years to enforce court judgments.

Because student loans are unsecured consumer debt, loan servicers should take appropriate steps to avoid loan defaults by borrowers. Delinquent loans should be actively managed and collections efforts effectively performed. Once loans enter the repayment phase, the servicers' main objectives are to collect payments, pursue delinquent accounts, and minimize loan defaults while providing effective customer service.

An effective student loan collection process is a key component of controlling and minimizing credit losses. Whether performed by a third party or in-house, the process should be guided by well-established policies and procedures and should be managed effectively at each stage for optimal and legal collection of principal and interest to occur. Private student loan servicers must adhere to the FDCPA, which prohibits abusive debt collection practices.

---

[56] Dodd–Frank establishes an ombudsman for student loans within the CFPB who is responsible for making "appropriate recommendations" to the CFPB Director, the Secretary of the Treasury, the Secretary of Education, and Congress.

[57] Refer to *Annual Report of the CFPB Student Loan Ombudsman*, 2012, 2013, and 2014.

[58] Refer to "State-by-State List of Statute of Limitations on Debt."

The problems associated with an inadequately managed collection function include

- reduced earnings caused by increased loan losses and reduced recoveries.
- inaccurate or untimely communications to senior management and the directorate.
- inaccurate reporting of past-due and charged-off loans, and imprudent management decisions.
- insufficient allowance for loan losses caused by weak MIS, inaccurate past due figures, and the improper use of deferment, forbearance, and other collection-related practices.
- inadequate audit trail of collection and recovery activities.
- poorly trained employees, resulting in loss of productivity, collections, and recoveries.
- violations of laws and regulations.

Technology

The loan collection function generally relies on automation and technology to be competitive, remain compliant, operate efficiently, and increase profitability. Banks and third parties generally use technology and historical information to formulate a plan or strategy for optimizing their collection efforts. Communication technology has grown in sophistication over time. This technology is used to leverage an integrated and multi-channel approach to borrower communication with voice alerts, outbound interactive voice response, predictive dialing, preview calling, e-mails, and custom websites. Even skip tracing techniques have evolved and use social media to locate borrowers. Whatever form of communication banks or third parties use to contact borrowers, privacy is a significant consideration. Banks must adhere to the FDCPA and other applicable laws and regulations, including state dialer and messaging restrictions, operator and consent rules, and rules addressing identification data blocks, drop rates, call times, and other subjects.

In contrast with communication technology used in the loan collection function, the infrastructure used to administer and service private student loans has limited functionality. These are generally legacy systems designed primarily to support repayment options offered in the federal guaranteed loan programs.[59] These platforms were not designed to accommodate TDR[60] analysis and financial reporting requirements. Consequently, some workout options for private student loans (e.g., restructuring or modifications) would likely require platform technology enhancements.

Examiners should have a general understanding of the technologies employed by in-house collection departments or third parties to evaluate their effectiveness. Bank management should appropriately oversee and govern third-party relationships, and there should be no

---

[59] Examples include the Graduated Repayment Plan, Income-Contingent Repayment Term, Extended Repayment, and Income-Based Repayment. Refer to appendix E of this booklet for more information.

[60] Accounting Standards Codification Subtopic 310-40 states that a TDR is "a restructuring in which a bank, for economic or other reasons related to a borrower's financial difficulties, grants a concession to the borrower that it would not otherwise consider." Accounting Standards Codification 310-40-15-9 states that a TDR includes "a modification of the loan terms, such as a reduction of the stated interest rate, principal, or accrued interest or an extension of the maturity date at a stated interest rate lower than the current market rate for new debt with similar risk."

gaps in banks' information technology risk management programs. If loan servicers are using work-arounds to adhere to requirements of TDR enhanced accounting and reporting, examiners should ensure that the banks have the appropriate internal controls.

Collection Strategies

Collection strategies determine which accounts are put in collection queues, the timing of collection activities, and the type of contact (e.g., phone calls, collection letters, and legal letters). Seasonality is a factor in private student loan collections. Borrowers who graduate in December begin repayment after the six-month grace period. That is why many accounts enter first payment default between May and June. By the same token, borrowers who graduate in May enter the collection queue in the fourth quarter of the year. Bank management should adjust its collection strategies and staffing to accommodate this seasonality.

Most banks with effective loan collection units engage in delinquency prevention. Some of the most common strategies they employ are the following:

- **Early withdrawal strategy:** Banks send high-level e-mails and perform outbound calls to borrowers who withdrew from school and provide counseling on repayment options during the grace period. The goal of the strategy is to reduce loan defaults for this population.
- **Pre-repayment strategy:** Banks generally make outbound calls to borrowers who recently graduated and borrowers coming out of forbearance. These calls educate customers on the amount and due date of their payments, methods of payment, and bank contact information (e.g., website, e-mail, phone number, and address). This strategy is also helpful in determining if skip tracing is necessary.

Another consideration in private student loan collection is borrower mobility. New graduates may move immediately after graduation or separation from school. Banks recognize that some student loan defaults result from failure to locate borrowers or otherwise having no contact with borrowers. Default and debt management programs can work only when banks can locate borrowers. Pre-repayment strategies that include soliciting updated borrower and cosigner information, including cellphone numbers, have proved to be effective. These efforts help borrowers transition from deferment and the grace period into making payments.

In many banks, collection strategies rely on behavior scoring models to segment accounts by risk. Transaction analytics also help in developing effective behavior score models that adapt or adjust to portfolio changes. High-risk accounts should have higher collection phone call attempts and customer contacts to increase likelihood of collection. Banks use behavior score models to predict likelihood of collection and to more precisely alter banks' actions and timing for collection activity. Banks use analytics and segmentation to determine not only the appropriate collection action but also whether to send accounts to third-party collection agencies and at what point to do so. Examiners should review and discuss with bank management the collection strategies and reports generated. Banks should maintain close control over their collection strategies and understand the impact of strategy changes to dollars collected.

Supervision of collection staff is important. Bank management should ensure that collection supervisors have appropriate collections experience and good management skills. Bank management should align incentives with collection goals and collector performance measures, and should require that collection supervisors regularly review the collectors' performance. Collection activities should be subject to regular quality assurance and internal audit review.

Internal Audit

Because of the variety of risks inherent in private student lending activities, internal audit coverage should include evaluating all the risks and controls in the bank's private student lending operations. The scope and frequency of these audits should be based on the risk of associated controls and complexity of banks' private student lending activities. Internal audit staff should be able to identify control breakdowns and ensure appropriate remediation. Internal audit should assess strategic business risks and the overall risk management framework, including complying with bank policies, approved practices and limits, and applicable laws and regulations. Internal audit staff should be independent and knowledgeable about private student lending activities.

Staff should report audit findings, including identified control weaknesses, to the board or a designated committee. The board and bank management should ensure that the internal audit staff has the necessary qualifications and expertise to review private student lending activities.

Risk Rating and Examiner Guidance

Classification and Charge-Off Policies

Private student loan account classification and charge-off practices are addressed in OCC Bulletin 2000-20, "Uniform Retail Credit Classification and Account Management Policy: Policy Implementation." In general, under this policy, private student loans that reach 90 days past due are classified "substandard," and loans that become 120 days past due are classified as a loss and charged off. The guidance includes special rules for bankrupt, fraudulent, and deceased borrower accounts, and examiners should review this bulletin closely before considering banks' collection activities.

For private student loans, just because loans are classified as a loss or charged off does not mean that the lender should stop using workout or modification programs or that loss mitigation or collection efforts should cease, unless prohibited by law. It simply means that for safety and soundness reasons and financial and investor transparency, banks should follow appropriate accounting practices.

MIS for Collections

The volume and trends in delinquencies and losses are central to evaluating collections and overall portfolio performance. Robust, timely MIS reporting identifies loans or portfolio segments that are not performing as expected and helps bank management understand portfolio quality. The bank's set of MIS reports on private student loans should give bank management a view of loans that are in repayment, as well as the range of loss mitigation and collection activities in which the bank engages. The reports should provide bank management with a comprehensive and accurate view of the portfolio's risk including tracking effectiveness of the bank's forbearance, workout, and modification programs.

Through bank MIS reports, bank management should be able to isolate key products, product combinations, and borrower characteristics to help understand which factors drive performance. Besides helping management track portfolio performance against expectations, bank MIS reports should assist in understanding policy limitations and enable management to benchmark against industry metrics.

MIS reports should not only support the collection process but also help ensure timely recognition of losses.

Because of the nature of student loans, there could be a significant time lag between the disbursement of loan funds and the start of repayment. Therefore, any private student loan MIS should provide portfolio metrics that clearly distinguish the account status (in repayment versus deferment).

Equally or even more important, MIS reports should help bank management understand the factors influencing portfolio performance (e.g., underwriting, marketing, and collection staffing). Understanding these factors promotes a more realistic assessment of portfolio performance as well as an accurate evaluation of the workload and effectiveness of the bank's collection function. MIS helps ensure that remedial actions implemented are properly constructed to address the problem rather than a symptom. For example, private student loan MIS should have appropriate segmentation and granularity necessary to monitor performance for each school or education program based on delinquencies and losses. This granularity of MIS reports helps bank management evaluate school relationships and terminate poorly performing relationships and programs when necessary.

The roll rate report,[61] for example, allows bank management to review the number and dollar volume of accounts that move from current to 30-days delinquent, 30- to 60-days, etc. This information helps management to predict the charge-off rate as far as six months into the future. In addition, this report can aid management decisions regarding collection staffing levels.

---

[61] Roll rates measure the movement of accounts and balances from one payment status to another (e.g., percentage of accounts or dollars that were current last month rolling to 30 days past due this month).

Examiners should evaluate the bank's MIS for timely, accurate, relevant, and effective information and should strongly criticize the absence of appropriate tracking and monitoring reports.

Workout Program and Debt Management

The Education Department allows several repayment and debt management[62] alternatives for financially distressed borrowers with federal student loans. These repayment alternatives include extended repayment plans such as graduated repayment, income-contingent repayment term, extended repayment, and income-based repayment. Debt forgiveness is another alternative. Some of these alternatives may not be appropriate for private student loans and may not be consistent with safe and sound banking principles. The Education Department defines federal student loan default as 270 days past due, compared with 120 days past due for banks' private student loans. The Education Department also allows loan deferment due to unemployment for a maximum of three years. These Education Department programs and practices have brought pressure to banks to align their repayment and workout programs for private student loans to those of federal student loans. Banks have some latitude to offer similar federal workout programs to private student loans. Banks, however, should do so while adhering to safety and soundness requirements and following existing banking guidance and GAAP.

Two OCC issuances provide guidance related to student loan deferment, forbearance, and modifications. First, OCC Bulletin 2000-20, "Uniform Retail Credit Classification and Account Management Policy: Policy Implementation," provides general guidance on classifying retail credits for regulatory purposes and establishing policies for working with borrowers experiencing temporary financial difficulties. Second, the examiner guidance, CNBE Policy Guidance 2010-2 (REV), "Policy Interpretation: OCC Bulletin 2000-20—Application to Private Student Lending," affirms the applicability and fundamental principles of the Retail Classification Policy to private student lending while recognizing the unique aspects of higher education financing.[63]

OCC Bulletin 2000-20 and CNBE Policy Guidance 2010-2 (REV) address supervisory expectations for risk management of loan workout programs and arrangements, classification of loans, and regulatory reporting and accounting considerations. Examiners and bankers should remember that workout programs can be used to help borrowers overcome temporary financial difficulties, if those actions

- do not cloud the true performance and delinquency status of the portfolio.
- are reported accurately for call report and financial reporting purposes.
- are based on the borrower's renewed willingness and ability to repay the loan.
- are structured and controlled in accordance with sound internal policies.

---

[62] Workout programs are commonly referred to as "debt management" in the student lending industry.

[63] This policy guidance previously was available only internally to OCC employees and is being made public with this booklet.

Bank management should note that regulatory agencies encourage financial institutions to work constructively with private student loan borrowers experiencing financial difficulties and should consider workout arrangements that increase the potential for such borrowers to repay private student loans whenever workout arrangements are economically feasible and appropriate.[64] Banks should adopt their own standards for workouts and modifications and monitor the effectiveness of those standards. Banks should provide clear and practical information to student loan borrowers that explains the options available, general eligibility criteria, the process for requesting workouts, and information on how to contact lenders or loan servicers.

There are several repayment assistance remedies unique to private student loans, some of which are described in this section.

Deferment

In-school deferment is a temporary postponement of payments while borrowers are attending school (enrolled at least half time). Repayment of private student loans generally begins 60 days after disbursement. Most borrowers opt for in-school deferment of principal and interest. During this period, the interest is capitalized and added to the principal balance of the loan. Repayment then begins six months after graduation, when borrowers are no longer enrolled in school, or when borrowers are enrolled less than half time. Banks tie the length of deferment to the expected completion time of borrowers' education programs. Deferment should not affect other terms of the loan, including maturity.

Six-month grace is a standard period after graduation or withdrawal from school during which no payment is required, as interest continues to be capitalized. This grace period is automatically granted to borrowers who leave school or drop below half time before repayment begins. This grace period is ordinarily granted without conditions or documentation of any hardship. During the grace period, banks should contact borrowers to counsel them on repayment terms, the repayment process, and repayment responsibilities to ensure orderly transition to repayment.

Forbearance and Extension

Forbearance permits borrowers to temporarily postpone making payments or reduce the amount of payments for a limited and specific period if borrowers are unable to make the scheduled loan payments for reasons including temporary financial hardship. Borrowers are liable for the interest that accrues on loans during the forbearance period. Forbearance is granted at banks' discretion. Private student loans with repayment terms of 10 years or greater may have no more than 12 months of payment forbearance over the loans' terms. Banks should establish a lesser limit for loans with terms of less than 10 years.

Banks should consider granting forbearances for private student loans in one- or two-month increments, with three- to six-month forbearance terms granted only in exceptional

---

[64] Refer to OCC, "Agencies Encourage Lenders to Work With Student Loan Borrowers," news release 2013-118, July 25, 2013.

circumstances. There should be a 12-month period of positive payment performance before borrowers are eligible for subsequent forbearance. The two types of forbearance that banks should consider as possible remedies for short-term borrower hardship are extended grace and extensions. Both forbearance actions are consistent with existing OCC guidance.

- Extended grace is the period immediately after the grace period during which borrowers experiencing financial hardship are allowed an additional grace period of up to six months. Extended grace may be granted with appropriate documentation and gives borrowers a total of up to 12 months after graduation or withdrawal from school to obtain employment (grace period plus extended grace period) and begin repayment.[65] Examiners should assess whether banks contact borrowers to document and support the hardship requiring this forbearance option, establish borrowers' commitment to repay the debt, and evaluate the reasonableness of borrowers' prospective repayment capacity after the extended grace period.
- Extension is a form of forbearance used to roll back the maturity of loans by a specified number of months (e.g., one or two months). Accounts are shown to be current upon granting extensions.

The extended grace period and all extensions should count toward the maximum lifetime allowable payment forbearance of no more than 12 months. The limits on extensions are calculated on a per-loan basis. Management should consider incremental approval of the extended grace period and document ongoing conversations with borrowers to determine if borrowers have established means to repay the debt. Banks should notify cosigners of the approval of any extended grace period or other payment forbearance.

Examiners should assess whether bank practices that defer the start of the repayment period are well controlled, supported, and documented to prevent the inappropriate deferral of loss recognition in problem situations. Short-term forbearance for temporary hardship is typically not considered a TDR. A determination, however, should be made if a TDR exists if the modification is significant to the term, contractual balance, or other characteristics of the loan, and consistent with GAAP.

Military Deferment and Forbearance

In the case of an in-school military deferment, members of the military attending school (enrolled at least half time) and called into active duty[66] or qualifying National Guard duty[67] should be allowed deferment in increments of 12 months (maximum of 36 months).

---

[65] CNBE Policy Guidance 2010-2 (REV), "Policy Interpretation: OCC Bulletin 2000-20—Application to Private Student Lending."

[66] The term "active duty" is defined in 10 USC 101(d)(1). Also refer to 10 USC 688 12301(a), 10 USC 688 12301(g), 10 USC 12302, and 10 USC 12304.

[67] Qualifying National Guard duty refers to activation, reassignment, and full-time duty in connection with war, contingency operation, or national emergency. Refer to 10 USC 12301. The term "National Guard duty" is defined in 10 USC 101(d)(1), 10 USC 101(d)(3), and 10 USC 101(d)(5).

Examiners should assess whether banks review borrowers' military status after each 12-month deferment term.

For borrowers who are out of school, in repayment status, and called into active duty or qualifying National Guard duty, banks may grant a similar 12-month deferment (maximum of 36 months) on an exception basis recognizing the borrowers' reduced capacity to repay.

For military deferment and forbearance, examiners should verify whether bank management

- checks active duty papers to confirm mobilization or call to active duty.[68]
- provides the borrower education and counseling that include disclosure of capitalization of interest and non-waiver of principal during forbearance to both borrowers and cosigners.
- monitors and tracks military forbearance granted with appropriate internal controls, MIS, and quality assurance.

Additionally, banks must follow laws and regulations, including the SCRA, that apply to service members. This law provides various civil protections and rights to service members. Among the protections is a 6 percent interest rate cap on pre-service debts[69] and restrictions on default judgments against members in active duty military service. The U.S. Department of Justice may pursue enforcement actions for SCRA claims against lenders through the agency's Civil Rights Division. Similarly, the OCC may consider what supervisory response, including taking an enforcement action, is appropriate if one of its supervised banks violates the SCRA.

Long-Term Hardship

Banks should work with borrowers experiencing long-term financial hardship in a constructive way. For long-term hardships, banks may temporarily or permanently offer workout programs that include modification or restructure. Private student loans, however, should not be treated differently from other retail loans. The terms of any workout programs should be consistent with the nature of borrowers' hardship, have sustainable payment requirements, and promote orderly, systematic repayment of amounts owed. Banks should structure workout terms based on borrowers' and cosigners' (if any) renewed willingness and ability to repay the loans. Banks should be cautioned against workouts that suspend repayment for protracted periods without sufficient documentation of borrowers' hardship or willingness and reasonably expected ability to repay. Workouts should be controlled in accordance with sound bank workout policies.

---

[68] Banks may review call to active duty beginning and end date or access the U.S. Department of Defense database.

[69] Pursuant to 50 USC 3937 (SCRA), "Maximum Rate of Interest on Debts Incurred Before Military Service," the term "interest" includes service charges, renewal charges, fees, or any other charges (except bona fide insurance) with respect to an obligation or liability.

For long-term hardships, banks may temporarily or permanently reduce the interest rate to lower borrowers' payments. Any temporary reduction in borrowers' interest rates should provide reasonable transitions back to the contract rate to avoid payment shock. Conversely, extensions of loan terms or allowing non-amortizing payments or balloon payments at maturity are generally not appropriate actions for long-term hardships because there has not been any demonstrated ability by borrowers to repay.

In determining whether to criticize banks with troubled private student loans, examiners should consider whether banks have offered appropriate modifications to borrowers, including restructured loans that result in adverse credit classifications or TDR under GAAP. By the same token, potential or actual treatment as a TDR should not prevent banks from proactively working with borrowers to restructure loans with reasonable modified terms. Consideration and evaluation of cosigners and guarantors should guide the decision and selection of the best borrower option. Any private student loan restructure should be supported by a current, well-documented credit evaluation of borrowers' and cosigners' (if any) financial condition and prospects for repayment under the revised terms.

Banks should evaluate whether restructured private student loans should be reported as a TDR. Not all modifications of loan terms, however, automatically result in a TDR. For example, if the modified terms are consistent with market conditions and representative of terms that borrowers could obtain in the open market given similar credit characteristics, the restructured loan is not considered a TDR.[70]

For reporting purposes, a restructured loan is considered a TDR when banks, for economic or legal reasons related to borrowers' financial difficulties, grant concessions to borrowers in modifying or renewing loans that the banks would not otherwise consider. Modifications of loan terms, such as extensions of the maturity date or reductions of the stated interest rate lower than the current market rate for new debt with similar risk, are considered concessions and qualify as a restructuring under GAAP. Private student loans that have undergone TDRs in compliance with their modified terms should be reported as restructured loans in schedule RC-C, part I, memorandum item 1, of the call report.

Additionally, banks should evaluate whether accrual of interest remains appropriate for private student loan TDRs. Non-accrual reporting status for individual private student loans is not specifically required, but banks should take steps to ensure that the net income is not materially overstated.

Guidance on reporting TDRs, including characteristics of modifications, is included in the Federal Financial Institutions Examination Council (FFIEC) call report instructions and OCC Bulletin 2012-10, "Troubled Debt Restructurings: Supervisory Guidance on Accounting and Reporting Requirements."

---

[70] *Bank Accounting Advisory Series*, Topic 2A, question 1, September 2015.

Examination Considerations

Standards, policies, and procedures: When examining banks' student lending workout programs, examiners should understand the different workout arrangements and determine if banks have prudent workout standards and eligibility criteria that control the use of and limit the number and frequency of forbearances, extensions, deferments, and modifications. The standards should prohibit any additional advances to finance unpaid interest and fees. Examiners should assess whether banks have

- standards, policies, and procedures that determine borrowers' financial condition and overall capacity to repay through evaluation of income, employment, and other debts.
- approval and reporting requirements.
- program eligibility criteria tailored toward borrowers' financial difficulty, including temporary, short-term, or long-term difficulty.

Examiners should assess bank practices by (1) reviewing the analysis that supports the banks' decision to offer workout arrangements, and (2) evaluating whether banks adhere to their standards, policies, and procedures. Examiners should evaluate whether banks consider the nature of borrower hardship and whether there is a reasonable basis to support repayment in the future. Examiners should sample several accounts to ensure that bank workout practices adhere to bank policy and that bank practices and policy are consistent with OCC guidance.

Documentation and MIS: Banks' decisions to grant deferment, forbearance, extension, modification, or any other workout arrangement should be supported in the banks' MIS. Bank documentation should show that there was communication between the borrowers and the banks and that borrowers have the ability to repay the loans. Examiners should review bank MIS and evaluate if banks have adequate MIS that identify and document any private student loans placed in workout programs, including the number of times such action has been taken.

Management oversight: There are risks in lax management supervision of workout programs, including accumulation of problem accounts and understatement of portfolio delinquencies, charge-offs, and provisions. Banks should control and manage the volume and complexity of workout programs including following regulatory reporting and GAAP requirements. Banks should have an allowance for loan and lease losses (ALLL) methodology that is consistent with GAAP and recognizes credit losses in a timely manner through provisions and charge-offs.

Management should monitor and track the volume and performance of loans that have been placed in workout arrangements and measure the effectiveness of programs over time (e.g., percentage of accounts that cure and charge off). The outcome should justify the practice. For workout programs to be effective, banks may consider

- tracking the 13-month rolling volume of loans (number and dollar amounts) that were placed into deferment, extension, forbearance, etc., by month and monitoring this long term (e.g., last three years).
- monitoring performance for each deferment or forbearance since the deferment or forbearance arrangement ended.
- tracking historical performance by repayment vintage and even grouping this by accounts that received different types of workout since entering repayment.
- monitoring average credit score of accounts in forbearance or repayment (dollar weighted) and comparing this with the average credit score for new volume.

Consolidation and Refinance

Some banks offer consolidation and refinance loans to borrowers who wish to simplify and streamline their repayment efforts. Consolidation allows borrowers to combine private student loans into single fixed-rate consolidation loans (or variable rate, if preferred), thus providing single due dates and billing statements. If primary borrowers' credit profiles have improved significantly, the primary borrowers may qualify for better rates and may remove the cosigners (if any) from individual loans. Consolidation and refinance may be used to switch lenders and enable borrowers to shop for the best possible loan term and pricing.

Banks should exercise caution when offering consolidation of both federal and private student loans. Borrowers who refinance federal student loans into private student loans may lose favorable benefits from the original federal student loans (e.g., Perkins loan subsidized interest and loan forgiveness). Banks may consider helping borrowers determine if consolidation provides the expected benefit.

In general, both federal and private student loans cannot be discharged in bankruptcy. Still, in determining whether student loans are protected against discharge (pursuant to 11 USC 523(a)(8)(B)), banks should consider whether the loans meet the definition of "qualified education loan."[71] The student loan debt should be incurred within "a reasonable period"[72] with the debt attributable to education furnished during a period in which the borrowers were eligible students.

Recoveries

Recoveries are collection activities after accounts are charged off. Student loans are rarely permitted to be discharged in bankruptcy, which allows lenders to pursue recoveries from borrowers for longer periods if banks seek and obtain court judgments against borrowers.

---

[71] A bankruptcy discharge exception is applied to qualified education loans in 11 USC 523(a)(8)(B), "Exceptions to Discharge."

[72] The term "reasonable period" is defined in 26 CFR 1.221-1(e)(3)(ii), "Deduction for Interest Paid on Qualified Education Loans After December 31, 2001."

Similar with other retail loan products, recovery activities for private student loans are generally conducted internally and may be outsourced to collection agencies after several months. Collection agencies receive a percentage of the dollars collected, and the percentage varies based on whether the agency is the primary (the first agency to work the accounts), secondary, or tertiary collector. The primary agency generally collects the lowest percentage, and the tertiary agency collects the highest percentage.

Some of the factors that may affect the recovery rate are

- previous collection efforts.
- depth and experience of staff.
- adequacy of systems and controls.
- use of technology.

When the bank selects an agency with which the bank will outsource accounts, the bank should perform appropriate due diligence to ensure that the agency is, among other things, properly licensed and bonded. The bank should have systems to monitor the agency continuously to ensure the agency is operating in a prudent manner. Bank management should follow the guidance outlined in OCC Bulletin 2013-29, "Third-Party Relationships: Risk Management Guidance," as the bank works with third parties to collect accounts.

Allowance and Capital Treatment

For performing private student loans, bank management should establish appropriate ALLL levels that consider the credit quality of the portfolios and conditions that affect collectability. Most banks provide for at least one year of projected losses for their consumer portfolios, though the coverage period may be shorter or longer based on portfolio characteristics and performance. If the methodology and assumptions used are sound, the analysis of the credit quality of the portfolios and conditions for collectability determines the appropriate level and coverage of ALLL. Banks that engage in private student lending activities must comply with the OCC's risk-based capital and leverage ratio requirements that apply to those activities.

All private student loans whose terms have been modified in a TDR should be evaluated for impairment under Accounting Standards Codification Topic 310-10. Private student loans that have been modified in a TDR are impaired when, based on analysis of current information and events, it is probable that the bank will be unable to collect all amounts due (i.e., both principal and interest) according to the contractual terms of the original loan agreements. When the review of impaired private student loans confirms that a specific restructured loan is uncollectable, the amount that is uncollectable should be charged off.

Banks with federal guaranteed student loan portfolios on their balance sheets should account for the portion of the loans not covered by the guarantee in the banks' ALLL and regulatory capital. When government-guaranteed loans become 120 days past due, a dollar-for-dollar reserve should be established for the unguaranteed portion and reported accurately for call report and financial reporting purposes. For the purposes of capital, the guaranteed portion of federal student loans is subject to a risk weight of 20 percent as a conditional guarantee of the U.S. government while the remaining unguaranteed 0 percent to 3 percent should be risk weighted at 100 percent. Private student loans that are 90 days past due have a general risk weight of 150 percent.[73]

For more information on allowance, refer to OCC Bulletin 2006-47, "Allowance for Loan and Lease Losses (ALLL): Guidance and Frequently Asked Questions (FAQs) on the ALLL," and the OCC's *Bank Accounting Advisory Series*.

Rehabilitated Federal Student Loans

Bank participation in the student lending industry is not simply confined to the "originate and hold" model. In the past few years, some community banks found new opportunities by purchasing pools ("buy and hold") of student loans in the Federal Rehabilitation Student Loan Program. The program is made up of federal student loans with borrowers who previously defaulted but have brought the loans current with nine consecutive payments.

Federal student loans generally fall into default after borrowers miss 270 days of loan payments (if payments are due monthly) or 330 days of loan payments (if payments are due less frequently).[74] The Education Department offers a federal student loan rehabilitation program to help borrowers bring education loans out of default through affordable payments. Rehabilitation is a one-time opportunity to remove a federal student loan default from a borrower's credit history and to regain student aid eligibility. To rehabilitate a federal student loan, the borrower must make nine on-time,[75] full monthly payments to the guarantor or its contracted vendor during a period of 10 consecutive months. Payments must be made voluntarily by the borrower and must be equal to or greater than the amount determined to be reasonable and affordable. The definition of "voluntary" in this context excludes payments made by garnishment or other offsets. After the borrower makes nine of 10 consecutive payments and applies for and receives "rehabilitation," the borrower will no longer be considered in default.

A rehabilitated loan retains the same interest rate and deferment provisions that were applicable when the loan was first disbursed and keeps repayment terms and all other benefits applicable to other federal student loans. The borrower, however, regains eligibility for deferment only to the extent that he or she has not already exhausted those deferment privileges before the initial default. For example, a borrower who was initially eligible for 24 months of unemployment deferment, and who used 12 months of that eligibility before his or her default, would be eligible to defer the rehabilitated loan for only 12 months due to any future unemployment status.

---

[73] Refer to 12 CFR 3, subpart D (12 CFR 3.30–3.63), "Risk-Weighted Assets–Standardized Approach." The OCC adopted the revised capital rules as final on July 9, 2013 (78 Fed. Reg. 62018 [October 11, 2013]).

[74] Refer to 34 CFR 682.200(b), "Definitions."

[75] The term "on-time payment" is defined as payments within 20 days of the due date for FFELP and Direct Loan Program loans and 15 days for Perkins loans.

Once loans are redeemed, they are removed from collections and either returned to the original federal student loan servicers or purchased by eligible lending institutions. Rehabilitation of FFELP loans usually requires that the loans be sold to lenders after the borrowers complete the steps required to rehabilitate the loans. Community banks that buy these pools of loans generally receive a 2 percent to 3 percent discount and use third parties for servicing and administration. This new business is attractive to community banks because the government guarantees 97 percent to 100 percent of the principal of each loan.

Rehabilitated FFELP loan pools are expected to have a higher net loss rate compared with pools of non-rehabilitated FFELP loans because, although the rehabilitated loans benefit from the same degree of federal guarantee, they are expected to default at a significantly higher rate than non-rehabilitated loans. Bank management should ensure that the bank is indemnified from any loan servicer errors and can adequately manage the risks, such as third-party, liquidity, interest rate, compliance, and reputation risk.

Examiners should assess whether banks that buy these pools have a thorough understanding of the risks associated with the portfolios. To most community banks, engaging in rehabilitated FFELP is a new activity. Community bank examiners should closely monitor how effectively banks manage this program.

Examination Procedures

This booklet contains expanded procedures for examining specialized activities or specific products or services that warrant extra attention beyond the core assessment contained in the "Community Bank Supervision," "Large Bank Supervision," and "Federal Branches and Agencies Supervision" booklets of the *Comptroller's Handbook*. Examiners determine which expanded procedures to use, if any, during examination planning or after drawing preliminary conclusions during the core assessment.

Scope

These procedures are designed to help examiners tailor the examination to each bank and determine the scope of the student lending examination. This determination should consider work performed by internal and external auditors and other independent risk control functions and by other examiners on related areas. Examiners need to perform only those objectives and steps that are relevant to the scope of the examination as determined by the following objective. Seldom will every objective or step of the expanded procedures be necessary.

The scope of student lending supervisory activities depends on the examiner's knowledge of those activities, the amount of total and product exposure, and the amount of risk posed to the bank's earnings and capital.

This booklet provides two sets of procedures: primary and supplemental.

The "Primary Examination Procedures" section in this booklet discusses the steps necessary for a comprehensive student lending examination in smaller or less complex operations and serves as the base student lending procedures for larger or more complex operations.

The "Supplemental Examination Procedures" section in this booklet discusses when examiners should expand the scope of the examination. For example, it may be necessary to supplement primary procedures when the bank offers new or significantly changed products, when a particular concern exists, or when examining larger, more complex operations. The supplemental examination procedures are grouped by functional areas. Examiners are encouraged to refer to other *Comptroller's Handbook* booklets, including the following:

- "Allowance for Loan and Lease Losses"
- "Community Bank Supervision"
- "Concentrations of Credit"
- "Internal and External Audits"
- "Internal Control"
- "Large Bank Supervision"
- "Loan Portfolio Management"
- "Rating Credit Risk"

In connection with evaluating compliance with applicable laws, examiners are also encouraged to refer to appropriate booklets in the *Consumer Compliance* series of the *Comptroller's Handbook,* such as the "Truth in Lending Act," "Other Consumer Protection Laws and Regulations," and "Fair Lending" booklets. Based on the facts and circumstances of each bank, examiners should select the appropriate expanded procedures, internal control questionnaire (ICQ), or verification procedures to supplement the minimum procedures.

While reviewing student lending activities, examiners should remain alert for lending practices and product terms that could indicate discriminatory, unfair, deceptive, abusive, or predatory issues.

Objective: To determine the scope of the examination of student lending and identify examination objectives and activities necessary to meet the bank's supervisory strategy needs.

1. Review the following sources of information and note any previously identified problems related to student lending that require follow-up:

    *   Supervisory strategy
    *   Examiner-in-charge's (EIC) scope memorandum
    *   The OCC's information system
    *   Previous reports of examination (ROE) and work papers
    *   Internal and external audit reports and work papers, including Education Department's lender servicer review report
    *   Bank management's responses to previous ROEs and audit reports
    *   Borrower complaints and litigation

2. Obtain the results of the Uniform Bank Performance Report and the OCC's Canary benchmark report.

3. Obtain and review the policies, procedures, and reports bank management uses to supervise student lending, including internal risk assessments.

4. In discussions with bank management, determine if there have been any significant changes (for example, in policies, processes, personnel, control systems, products, volumes, markets, and geographies) since the previous examination of student lending.

5. Based on an analysis of information obtained in the previous steps, as well as EIC input, determine the scope and objectives of the student lending examination.

6. In preparing for the student lending examination, write a request letter as directed by the EIC (refer to this booklet's appendix B, "Sample Request Letter").

7. Select from the following primary and supplementary examination procedures the necessary steps to meet examination objectives and the supervisory strategy.

Primary Examination Procedures

The primary examination procedures provide the steps necessary for a comprehensive student lending examination in smaller or less complex operations and serve as the base student lending procedures for larger or more complex operations. The procedures include in-depth portfolio analysis and testing to promote examiners' assessments of the quantity, aggregate level, and direction of credit risk.

Note: If the National Credit Tool is available, examiners are encouraged to use the standard retail reports and the tool's other capabilities (i.e., custom reports and sampling) to assist in the student lending examination procedures.

Objective: To assess the level of risk, evaluate the quality of risk management, and determine the aggregate level and direction of risk of the bank's student lending activities.

1. Review the scope, conclusions, and work papers from previous supervisory activities. Determine the adequacy and timeliness of management's response to the issues identified and any findings or issues requiring follow-up.

2. Review relevant reports issued by internal and external audit, quality assurance, loan review, risk management, and compliance management since the previous supervisory activity. Determine the adequacy and timeliness of management's responses to the issues identified and any findings or issues requiring follow-up. Request work papers, if warranted.

3. Review the minutes of student lending-related management and board meetings conducted since the previous supervisory activity.

4. Obtain copies of complaints filed with the OCC (complaints reported to the Customer Assistance Group) and the CFPB (using the Consumer Complaint Database), and bank consumer complaint logs. Evaluate the information for significant issues and trends.

   Note: Complaints serve as a valuable early warning indicator for compliance, credit, and operational issues, including discriminatory, unfair, deceptive, abusive, and predatory practices.

5. Determine whether there is any litigation, either filed or anticipated, associated with student lending activities and the expected cost or other implications.

6. Develop an initial assessment of the quality and performance of the student lending portfolio and product segments using portfolio reports, risk management analyses, and the Uniform Bank Performance Reports. Consider

   • growth.
   • portfolio mix and changes.

- significance of the portfolio and each of the products in terms of total loans, total assets, and capital.
- credit performance.
- contribution to earnings and income composition (e.g., interest and fees).

If the bank securitizes assets, analyze data on a managed basis. Coordinate findings and conclusions with the examiner(s) assigned to review securitizations throughout the examination.

7. Discuss with management any changes made since the previous supervisory activity or planned for student lending products and operations, including

- growth overall and in individual products.
- portfolio product mix.
- off-balance-sheet retail credit activities (e.g., securitization activities).
- new products.
- terms on existing products.
- marketing or acquisition channels (e.g., direct mail, telemarketing, Internet, and third-party originators).
- expansion into new market and trade areas.
- new or expanded third-party loan generation or servicing arrangements.
- underwriting, risk selection criteria, and portfolio quality.
- monitoring and risk management processes.
- models used to underwrite or manage the portfolio, if any.
- retail loan systems, including underwriting, servicing, and collection platforms.

It is important to understand how management assesses the effects of changes on profitability and risk profile and how management incorporates the effects of changes into the planning and risk management processes.

Discuss management's perception of the competition and whether the bank can be successful in its market without changes. Determine the extent to which the changes made or proposed were in response to the competitive environment and the reasonableness of and analytical support for those changes.

8. Evaluate student lending management and the planning process. Specifically,

- determine whether student lending objectives are consistent with the bank's strategic plan and whether the objectives are reasonable in light of the bank's resources, expertise, capital support, product offerings, and competitive environment.
- determine whether the student lending marketing plans and budgets are consistent with the retail credit objectives and the bank's strategic plan.
- evaluate the adequacy of the student lending planning process (internal limits, growth, financial, and product-related), including the adequacy and timeliness of revisions when warranted by portfolio performance and new developments.

- determine management's risk appetite with respect to risk and return objectives (e.g., return on assets, return on equity, or return on investment) or credit performance hurdles (e.g., delinquency, credit loss, or risk score tolerances).
- assess the qualifications, expertise, and staffing levels of management and staff in view of existing and planned student lending activities.

9. Review and assess the adequacy of the bank's policies, procedures, and practices. Specifically,

- determine whether the board of directors approves the student loan policies at inception and includes those policies in its annual policy reviews thereafter.
- identify significant changes in underwriting criteria and terms. Determine
  - the effect of those changes on the portfolio and its performance.
  - whether underwriting policies provide appropriate guidance on assessing both the borrower's and the cosigner's capacity to repay the loan.
  - that capacity to repay includes consideration of income, financial resources, and debt service obligations.
- if the bank uses credit scoring models (e.g., bureau, pooled, or custom),
  - determine how the bank ensures that the model is appropriate for the target population and product offering.
  - assess the reasonableness of the process used to establish cutoffs and determine whether management changed the cutoffs between examinations and the implications for portfolio quality and performance.
  - determine whether the policy provides for model monitoring and validation.
- determine how policies and policy changes are communicated to staff, and assess the adequacy of the process.
- evaluate the bank's process for establishing policy exception criteria and limits, and for monitoring and approving underwriting policy exceptions (e.g., underwriting standards, loan terms, score overrides, and income documentation).
- determine the control processes used to track and monitor policy adherence (e.g., quality assurance, MIS reports, loan review, and audit), and assess the adequacy of those processes.
- if the bank uses third parties for such services as loan origination or collection, determine
  - how policies are communicated to those entities.
  - the adequacy of the processes for monitoring and reporting policy adherence and performance.
- determine whether the bank's policies and procedures, including those for third parties, provide adequate guidance to avoid discriminatory, unfair, deceptive, predatory, and abusive lending practices[76] (e.g., misleading disclosures).

---

[76] For more information, refer to the "Fair Lending" booklet of the *Comptroller's Handbook;* OCC Advisory Letters 2002-3, "Guidance on Unfair or Deceptive Acts or Practices," and 2003-2, "Guidelines for National Banks to Guard Against Predatory and Abusive Lending Practices"; and OCC Bulletin 2014-42, "Interagency Guidance Regarding Unfair or Deceptive Credit Practices."

10. Evaluate the condition and risk profile of the portfolio and individual products by reviewing historical trends and current levels of key performance indicators, such as loan balances, delinquencies, losses, recoveries, and profitability. Focus on dollar balance percentages but also consider percentages of numbers of accounts. Review performance indicators for

    - major products, sub-products, portfolio segments, acquisition channels, and acquired portfolios.
    - third-party originators.
    - internal performance indicator hurdles and metrics. Compare actual performance indicators with internally established objectives.
    - industry and peers, as available (e.g., industry organization, rating agency, and securitization research). Compare industry indicators with bank performance.

    In addition to coincident analysis,[77] consider performing vintage analysis,[78] especially if underwriting criteria, loan terms, or economic conditions have changed, and if the portfolio exhibits significant growth. If available and well maintained, the bank's chronology log[79] should prove useful in determining the causes of variances.

11. Review new account application volumes, approval rates, and booking rates to assess portfolio growth. Review new account metrics to determine the composition and quality of accounts currently being booked. Compare the quality of recent account bookings with that of accounts booked in the past. Metrics evaluated should include credit score distributions (if used), price tiers, payment-to-income ratios, debt-to-income ratios, geographic distribution, override volume, and credit policy exceptions.

12. Evaluate the expected performance of the portfolio and the individual products through analysis of management reports, portfolio segmentation, and discussions with management. Specifically, review

    - score distributions and trends for accounts over time, evaluating scores at application (e.g., application score and bureau score), refreshed bureau scores, and behavior scores.
    - delinquencies and losses by credit score range for each major scoring model and determine whether there has been any deterioration of the good-to-bad odds.
    - loan growth sources (e.g., branch, region, loan officer, and product channel, such as direct-to-consumer, school channel, telemarketing, direct mail, or Internet), and differences in performance by source.

---

[77] Coincident analysis relies on end-of-period reported performance, e.g., delinquencies or losses in relation to total outstandings of the same date.

[78] Vintage analysis groups loans by origination (vintage) for analysis purposes. Performance trends are tracked for each vintage and compared with other vintages of similar age (time on book).

[79] The chronology log is a sequential record of internal and external events relevant to the credit function.

- levels and trends of policy documentation exceptions, and the comparison of performance of accounts with exceptions versus overall portfolio.
- volumes and trends of first and early payment defaults.
- management's loss forecasts.

13. Review collection department reports and activities to determine the implications for credit quality.

    Note: Several of the procedures already performed reflect collections activities (e.g., review of delinquencies and losses).

    - Review roll rate[80] reports overall and by product; evaluate trends; and, if peer group performance is available, compare roll rates. Refer to appendix D of this booklet for more information on roll rates.
    - Review criteria, volume, performance, and trends for forbearance and other workout programs as well as for deferments, extensions, and restructures.
    - Determine the reasonableness of the bank's collection strategies and the adequacy and timeliness of the processes for making revisions.
    - Review the loss forecasting process and determine whether it is reasonable and reliable.

14. Assess the adequacy of MIS and reports used to provide management with the necessary information to monitor and manage all aspects of student lending. Determine whether

    - adequate processes exist to ensure data integrity and report accuracy, and balances and trends included in management's student lending reports reconcile with the bank's general ledger and with the call report.
    - various department reports are consistent, i.e., the reports show the same numbers for the same categories and time periods regardless of the unit generating the report.
    - descriptions of key management reports are maintained and updated.
    - reports are produced to track volume and performance by product, channel, and marketing initiative, and whether those reports support any test with implications for credit quality or performance (e.g., pricing, credit score cutoff, school, or program). This reporting process should be fully operational before the bank offers new products or initiates tests to accurately monitor performance from inception.
    - MIS and reports are available to clearly track volumes, performance, and trends for all types of forbearance and workout programs as well as activities including extensions, deferments, restructures, and modifications.
    - reports are clearly labeled and dated.

15. Determine whether the amount of ALLL is appropriate and whether the method of calculating the allowance conforms with GAAP. Assess whether management routinely analyzes the portfolio to identify instances when the performance of a product or segment

---

[80] Roll rates measure the movement of accounts and balances from one payment status to another (e.g., percentage of accounts or dollars that were current last month rolling to 30 days past due this month).

of a portfolio (e.g., workout programs) varies significantly from the performance of the overall portfolio. Any variation in performance should be adequately incorporated into the allowance analysis. Refer to the "Allowance for Loan and Lease Losses" booklet of the *Comptroller's Handbook* for guidance and specifically consider

- whether estimates and assumptions are documented and supported consistent with FFIEC guidance (OCC Bulletin 2001-37, "Policy Statement on Allowance for Loan and Lease Losses Methodologies and Documentation for Banks and Savings Institutions: ALLL Methodologies and Documentation").
- credit quality, including any changes to underwriting, account management, or collections that could affect future performance and credit losses.
- historical credit performance and trends (e.g., delinquency roll rates and flow-to-loss) overall, by product, and by vintage within products.
- level, trends, and performance of higher-risk populations (e.g., for-profit institutions).
- level, trends, and performance of cure or workout programs, including deferment, forbearance, extension, modification, and restructure.
- charge-off practices and consistency with OCC Bulletin 2000-20, "Uniform Retail Credit Classification and Account Management Policy: Policy Implementation," and CNBE Policy Guidance 2010-2 (REV), "Policy Interpretation: OCC Bulletin 2000-20—Application to Private Student Lending."
- whether management provides for accrued interest and fees deemed uncollectible in the allowance or in a separate reserve.
- the effects of securitization activities, if applicable.
- economic conditions and trends.

16. Validate the preliminary risk assessment conclusions by conducting on-site transaction testing. The purpose of working these samples includes verifying adherence to bank policies; determining whether the bank maintains adequate documentation of analysis and decisions; verifying whether MIS reports accurately capture exception information; and determining whether practices are inconsistent with bank policy or are not adequately depicted in existing management reports. The sample selected should be sufficient in size to reach a supportable conclusion.

    Examiners conducting testing should remain alert for potential discriminatory, unfair, deceptive, abusive, and predatory lending. If weaknesses or concerns are found, consult the bank's EIC or compliance examiner.

    For each product being reviewed,

    - sample recently approved loans to assess adherence to underwriting policy. If the bank uses credit scoring, select two samples: one sample from loans not automatically approved (e.g., judgmental decision involved even if credit scoring is used as a tool) and one sample from loans automatically approved.
    - sample recent "override" loans, i.e., exceptions to normal underwriting standards, to evaluate the adequacy and consistency of the judgmental decision process.

- sample loans that were 60 days or more delinquent two months ago and that are now current to determine whether the borrower cured the delinquency by making payments or whether the loan was extended or granted forbearance. If the latter, determine whether the action was consistent with existing bank policy and whether it complied with CNBE Policy Guidance 2010-2 (REV), "Policy Interpretation: OCC Bulletin 2000-20—Application to Private Student Lending."
- sample loans that were recently extended, deferred, renewed, or rewritten for compliance with bank policy and reasonableness. Compliance with bank policy should be judged against the bank's normal underwriting guidelines with respect to debt-to-income, amortization period, debt or payment limitations, and pricing.
- sample recently charged-off loans and review the borrower, payment, and collection history to determine whether the actions taken pre-charge-off were reasonable or if the practices simply had the effect of deferring losses.

Based on the results of transactional testing and the severity of concerns identified, determine whether the sample should be expanded. (**Note:** Refer to appendix A, "Transaction Testing," in this booklet for additional testing suggestions.)

17. Complete the "Uniform Retail Credit Classification and Account Management Policy" checklist in appendix C of this booklet to determine the bank's level of compliance with OCC Bulletin 2000-20, "Uniform Retail Credit Classification and Account Management Policy: Policy Implementation."

18. If the bank is involved in higher-risk student lending, regardless of whether formally designated as subprime, assess whether management realistically identifies the level of risk assumed and that the allowance and capital provide sufficient support for the activity.

    In addition, OCC Bulletin 1999-10, "Subprime Lending Activities," and OCC Bulletin 1999-15, "Subprime Lending: Risks and Rewards," provide guidance on policies and procedures. If the bank has a targeted subprime program with volume exceeding 25 percent of tier 1 capital, review adherence to the requirements of OCC Bulletin 2001-6, "Expanded Guidance for Subprime Lending Programs."

19. If the bank relies on third-party relationships for significant functions, review compliance with OCC Bulletin 2013-29, "Third-Party Relationships: Risk Management Guidance."

20. Determine the effectiveness of the loan review process for student lending. Determine the scope and frequency of the reviews and whether loan review provides a risk assessment of the quality of risk management and quantity of risk for student lending.

    Note: Refer to the "Conclusions" section in this booklet to complete the assessment and the exam.

21. Review copies of the materials provided to the board of directors and relevant senior management committees to determine if they are aware of the condition of the student

loan portfolio. These persons should be apprised of significant decisions that affect the quality and performance of the portfolio.

22. Fully document findings, conclusions, and recommendations in a memorandum for review and approval by the loan portfolio management examiner or the EIC. Reach a conclusion on the quality of risk management and the quantity, aggregate level, and direction of risk, and include all necessary support. To accomplish these ends, complete the following procedures:

- Determine whether further work needs to be completed in the student lending area to fully assess credit or other risks. If so, refer to the appropriate supplemental procedures.
- Provide asset totals to the EIC. In addition to the delinquency-based classifications outlined in the FFIEC Uniform Retail Credit Classification and Account Management Policy, consider bankruptcies, workout programs, and any other segments that meet the classified definitions.
- Provide student lending conclusions to the examiner responsible for assessing earnings and capital adequacy.
- If the bank securitizes assets, provide conclusions and supporting information about credit quality to the examiner assigned to review securitizations.
- If significant violations of laws or regulations are noted, prepare write-ups for inclusion in the ROE.
- Prepare a recommended supervisory strategy for the student lending area.
- Document findings in OCC systems as appropriate.

Supplemental Examination Procedures

The supplemental examination procedures provide the steps necessary to expand the scope of the review. Examiners may need to follow these steps to supplement the primary procedures when the bank offers new or significantly changed products, when a particular concern exists, or when examining more complex operations. The supplemental examination procedures are organized by functional areas.

Marketing and Account Acquisition

Objective: To determine whether student lending marketing activities are consistent with the bank's business plans, strategic plans, and risk appetite, and that appropriate controls and systems are in place before the bank rolls out new products or new-product marketing initiatives.

1. Assess the structure and expertise of the marketing department, focusing on management, key personnel, and staffing adequacy.

2. Review the bank's marketing plan and assess it for reasonableness given the bank's strategic plan and objectives, level of expertise, capacity (operational and financial resources), market area, and competition.

   - Determine whether the bank bases its plan on internally or externally prepared market, economic, or profitability studies. If external studies are used, obtain and review copies of those studies.
   - Review the process for developing and implementing marketing plans, with particular attention to whether the appropriate functional areas (e.g., risk management, finance, operations, information technology, legal, and compliance) are involved throughout the process.
   - Assess the appropriateness of the data and assumptions used to develop marketing plans, in part through the review of MIS reports that track actual performance against marketing plans.
   - Discuss with management the controls in place to monitor marketing plans and activities.

   Note: Before implementing any marketing initiative, including the rollout of a new product or change to an existing product, management should review all marketing materials, consumer disclosures, product features, and terms to identify and address potential discriminatory, unfair, deceptive, abusive, and predatory lending practices.[81]

   - Discuss with management any significant changes made or planned to the bank's account acquisition, account management, and cross-selling strategies, including changes in channels and the use of third parties.

---

[81] For more information, refer to the "Fair Lending" booklet of the *Comptroller's Handbook* and OCC Advisory Letter 2002-3, "Guidance on Unfair or Deceptive Acts or Practices," March 22, 2002.

3. Assess new product development. Specifically,

- discuss with management the new product development process.
- determine whether there are written guidelines for what constitutes a new product.
- review new product proposals and plans approved since the last examination.
- determine whether the appropriate functional areas (e.g., risk management, finance, operations, information technology, legal, and compliance) are involved throughout the development process to ensure that associated risks are properly identified and controlled. Determine whether the constituents remain involved during implementation.
- evaluate systems planning to determine whether MIS and reporting needs are adequately researched and developed before new products are rolled out. Determine whether the systems and reports are adequate to supervise and administer new products.
- evaluate the adequacy of the review and approval processes for new products.
- determine whether management, including appropriate legal and compliance personnel, reviews marketing materials during product development and implementation to avoid deceptive or misleading advertising, terms, and disclosures.
- determine whether the planning process adequately identifies and addresses the risks, operational needs, and systems support associated with different solicitation methods and channels, including direct applications, school applications, loan-by-phone, and the Internet.

4. Evaluate the adequacy of the bank's testing process for new products, marketing campaigns, and other significant initiatives. Review the process to assess whether testing

- is a required step for any new products or significant marketing and account management initiatives.
- is properly approved. Senior management should approve the testing plan and determine that the proposed test is consistent with the bank's strategic plan and meets strategic objectives.
- requires clear descriptions of test objectives and methods (e.g., assumptions, test size, selection criteria, and duration) as well as key performance measurements and targets.
- includes a strong test and control discipline. The test should include a clean holdout group and test groups that are not subject to any significant account management or cross-selling initiatives for the duration of the test. Strict test group design enables management to draw more accurate performance conclusions.
- is accorded an adequate period of time, sufficient to determine probable performance and to work through any operational or other issues. When the test involves a significant departure from existing bank products or practices, test duration should probably be longer. Tests generally should run at least six months and usually should run nine or 12 months. The time frame may vary depending on the product or practice being tested.
- is supported by appropriate MIS and reporting before implementation.
- requires a thorough and well-supported postmortem analysis in which results are presented to and approved by senior management and the board before full rollout.

5. Determine whether management assesses how underwriting standards for the new products may affect credit risk and the bank's risk profile.

6. Evaluate cross-selling strategies, including the criteria used to select accounts.

7. If the bank maintains a data warehouse, determine how it is used for marketing purposes and if it is capable of aggregating customer loan relationships.

8. Determine the adequacy and effectiveness of the bank's controls regarding information sharing, for both affiliates and unrelated third parties.

9. Prepare profiles for each of the products offered. Address

   - product description, including any unique characteristics and a general overview of terms (including pricing), target market (credit quality and geographic), and distribution channels.
   - changes in the product characteristics since the last examination.
   - volume and trends, discussing growth to date and planned.

10. Select at least one new product introduced since the previous supervisory activity to assess the bank's planning process. Specifically, review

    - the planning documents and the final approved proposal.
    - tests and analyses conducted, including performance compared to expectations.
    - MIS tracking reports.
    - available risk management, quality assurance, and audit reviews.
    - any subsequent product modifications and the basis and documented support for those changes.
    - management review and approval documentation.
    - information presented to the board of directors.

11. Develop conclusions about whether marketing activities are consistent with the bank's business plans, strategic plans, and risk appetite, and comply with applicable laws and regulations. Determine if appropriate controls and systems are in place before new products or marketing initiatives are rolled out.

Underwriting

Objective: To assess the quality of the bank's new student loans and any changes from past underwriting; determine the adequacy of and adherence to student lending policies and procedures; determine compliance with applicable laws and regulations; and gain a thorough understanding of the processes employed in account origination.

1. Ascertain and evaluate the types of student loans that the bank offers and evaluate the reasonableness of the following:

- Loan products offered and planned.
- Underwriting standards and terms.
- Degree of innovation (e.g., new terms, products, and markets).
- Markets served and economic conditions.
- Competitive environment.
- Volume and proportion of loan portfolio (managed and on book), by product.
- Level of participation in high-risk student lending.
- Types of marketing and account acquisition channels.
- Historical and planned growth.
- Securitization activities.

Note: When evaluating lending activities, examiners should remain alert for practices and product terms that could indicate potentially discriminatory, unfair, deceptive, abusive, or predatory practices.

2. Review new account metrics to determine the composition and quality of accounts currently being booked and the adequacy of MIS used to track new loan volume. Compare the quality of recent bookings to the quality of accounts booked in the past. Metrics evaluated, by product, should include

- application volume, and approval and booking rates.
- distribution of credit scores, if used, by applications, approved and booked.
- percentage of accounts with a cosigner.
- composition of loans booked by school type (i.e., graduate school, four-year college, technical school, for-profit institution, etc.).
- price tiers and fees.
- geographic distribution.
- override volume.
- credit policy exceptions.

3. Obtain an overview of the origination process and the steps involved. When describing the process in the work papers, document the following

- Which aspects of the underwriting process are automated versus manual?
- Use of credit scoring models (e.g., types of models, history of model use, monitoring, and validation).
- Differences in the underwriting processes arising from the application channel (i.e., direct to consumer, telemarketing, Internet, and school), and the differences for unsolicited versus prescreened applications.

4. Determine how management evaluates underwriter performance, including MIS for monitoring underwriter performance, and transaction testing completed by the underwriter manager for quality assurance.

5. If the bank uses credit scoring in the underwriting process, assess the mix of automated and judgmentally approved loans. Refer to the credit scoring steps in the "Risk Management and Control Functions" section of the "Supplemental Examination Procedures."

6. For banks that lend in multiple geographic areas or states, confirm that management performs periodic bureau preference analyses to determine optimal credit bureaus for different states or localities.

7. Obtain a copy of the bank's lending policies and procedures. Assess the adequacy and soundness of the policies and procedures, focusing on the main criteria used in the decision-making process and, if applicable, the verification processes used to confirm application and transaction information. Evaluate

   - permissible types of loans.
   - lending authority and limits, and the exception approval process.
   - limits on concentrations of credit (e.g., product and school type).
   - credit underwriting criteria, including measurements of the borrower and cosigner capacity to repay the loan (e.g., debt-to-income and payment-to-income ratios) and treatment of derogatory credit bureau items.
   - credit scorecard cutoffs and tolerances for overrides.
   - borrower credit grade definitions (e.g., A, B, and C).
   - repayment terms (e.g., duration, amortization schedule, and pricing).
   - exception and override processes, criteria, and tracking.

8. Determine whether the policies and procedures provide adequate guidance to avoid discriminatory, unfair, deceptive, abusive, and predatory lending practices. If weaknesses or concerns are found, consult the bank's EIC or compliance examiner.

   Note: For additional information, refer to the "Fair Lending" booklet of the *Comptroller's Handbook* and OCC Advisory Letter 2002-3, "Guidance on Unfair or Deceptive Acts or Practices."

9. Assess the adequacy of the process for changing underwriting standards. Review all changes in standards since the last examination, and determine their effect on the quality of the loan portfolio.

   - Review analyses and documentation supporting recent changes to underwriting criteria and score cutoffs.
   - Discuss reasons for changes (if not readily apparent) with bank management and determine whether there has been a shift in the credit risk appetite.
   - Determine whether all affected functional areas provide input to underwriting changes.
   - Verify that management maintains a chronology of significant changes to underwriting standards.

10. Determine the adequacy of the bank's verification procedures and verify that, at a minimum, residence, employment, income, and school certification are routinely confirmed for borrowers.

11. Evaluate credit policy exception and scorecard override limits, tracking, and reporting. Determine whether

    - volumes conform to policy limits, and that those limits are reasonable.
    - management tracks the volumes and trends of policy exceptions (by type) and overrides separately and by reason code.
    - management tracks the performance (i.e., delinquencies and losses) of these accounts over time, by type, and compares the performance to that of the overall portfolio.
    - as warranted, management responds appropriately to the levels of overrides and exceptions, adjusting underwriting policies and exception limits or providing additional underwriter training accordingly.
    - management appropriately identifies the effects of the levels of exceptions and overrides and the performance of affected accounts on the quantity and direction of credit risk.

12. Select and test appropriate loan samples to determine credit quality; to verify adherence to bank underwriting policies, including verification procedures; to assess the adequacy of analysis and decision documentation; to ensure compliance with laws and regulations; to determine that MIS reports accurately capture exception information; and to determine whether practices exist that are inconsistent with bank policy or that are not adequately depicted in existing management reports. If the underwriting is outsourced, obtain the bank's on-site monitoring reports for third-party underwriting. The bank should be sampling and re-underwriting loans to ensure the third party is following the bank's underwriting guidelines. For each significant product type,

    - sample recently approved loans to assess adherence to underwriting policy and applicable laws and regulations. If the bank uses credit scoring, select two samples: one sample from loans not automatically approved (e.g., judgmental decision involved even if credit scoring is used as a tool) and one sample from loans automatically approved. Ensure that your sample includes loans originated from each significant marketing channel and, if warranted, consider expanding the sample to more thoroughly test specific channels.
    - sample recently approved loans that represent exceptions to underwriting policy to determine whether credit decisions are consistent, whether the analysis and other support for them is adequate, and whether the exceptions are approved on a non-prohibited basis.

      Use the bank's credit files, account origination systems, and MIS reports to create a worksheet to summarize information for the sample. The worksheet should be tailored to fit the product and the bank's underwriting criteria but generally includes the following information

- Account data: name, account number, origination date, employment information, time at residence, cosigner.
- Underwriting terms: credit score (bureau, pooled, or custom), debt-to-income, payment-to-income, interest rate, loan term, payment amount.
- Underwriting policy exceptions and score overrides (indicate whether bank or examiner identified).

If prepared properly, the worksheet facilitates examiner analysis and provides a sound foundation for reaching conclusions about the adequacy of the bank's policy and adherence to it.

Note: Examiners should follow OCC internal policy in handling personally identifiable information.

13. Based on the results of the testing and the severity of the concerns identified, determine whether the samples should be expanded. Refer to appendix A for additional sample suggestions.

14. Develop conclusions on the quality of the bank's new loans, any changes from past underwriting, the adequacy of and adherence to student lending policies and procedures, compliance with applicable laws and regulations, the processes employed in account origination, MIS for monitoring new loan volume, and implications for the risk profile of the loan portfolio. Clearly document all findings.

Loan Servicing and Administration

Objective: To assess the effectiveness of activities associated with student loan servicing and administration; determine whether student loan servicing and administrative activities are executed in compliance with applicable laws, regulations, board-approved strategy, and consistency with guidance; and to evaluate whether student loan servicing and administrative activities enhance performance of existing, nondelinquent accounts or portfolios.

1. Determine whether the board of directors or its designated banking committee has adopted student lending policies that appropriately cover all facets of the servicing and administration operation.

2. Determine whether the bank verifies the borrower's in-school status. If so, assess the adequacy of the process, including the policies and procedures employed.

3. Review policies and procedures in place to ensure the accuracy and integrity of information furnished to consumer reporting agencies.

4. Evaluate the adequacy of the bank's process for approving and communicating approval of private student loans.

5. Determine whether bank systems are capable of aggregating the entire loan relationship

by customer (multiple loan accounts by product and in total) for the purpose of customer-level account management. If so, determine the extent to which the bank uses that capability.

6. Determine whether the bank provides both the borrower and cosigners with necessary information and disclosures during the application, approval, and closing process.

7. Assess the adequacy of the bank's processes when the borrower is transitioning to repayment.

8. Determine whether the bank provides the borrower and cosigners with information associated with different repayment options before the loan becomes due or before repayment begins. If so, evaluate the adequacy of the process, including the timing of the notification, information provided (i.e., online), and other tools and options provided to help the borrower manage repayment of the loan.

9. Assess the bank's policies and procedures, internal controls, and training regarding identifying and following all repayment options.

10. Determine whether the bank has retained appropriate documentation of all benefits offered to the borrower and whether the bank has sufficient controls to ensure that rules on earned benefits are followed.

11. Determine whether the bank provides borrowers with periodic statements of the account. If so, examiners should review policies, procedures, and systems to assess the adequacy of statements that are provided to borrowers.

12. Determine whether the bank will renew, modify, or rewrite existing loans to nondelinquent customers. If so, evaluate the adequacy of the process, including the policies and procedures employed and the volume, trends, and subsequent performance of those loans.

Collections

Objective: To evaluate the effectiveness of the student lending collection function, including the collection strategies and programs employed, to better assess the quality of the portfolio and the quantity and direction of credit risk.

1. Assess the structure, management, and staffing of the collections department. If not previously performed,

   - review the organization chart for the department and evaluate the quality and depth of the staff based on the size and complexity of the operation.
   - discuss with senior management staffing plans for each major collection activity, such as early stage, late stage, fraud, and agency-management third-party collection,

including how plans fit with department and bank objectives (e.g., growth and credit performance projections).

- review the experience of senior managers and supervisors.
- assess the adequacy of the bank's training program for collectors through discussions with management.
- assess the appropriateness and administration of the bank's incentive pay program for collectors. Pay particular attention to possible negative ramifications of the plan, such as the potential to encourage protracted repayment plans, aggressive curing of accounts, or individual rather than team efforts. Determine whether the plan limits the total incentive pay that a collector can receive.
- determine whether the board or senior management reviewed and approved the incentive pay program before implementation.

2. Assess the adequacy of the bank's written collection policies and procedures. Determine whether they cover all significant collection activities and are consistent with OCC Bulletin 2000-20, "Uniform Retail Credit Classification and Account Management Policy: Policy Implementation," and CNBE Policy Guidance 2010-2 (REV), "Policy Interpretation: OCC Bulletin 2000-20—Application to Private Student Lending." Refer to the checklist in appendix C of this booklet.

- Verify that the bank's policies prohibit the rebooking of accounts that are charged off for anything other than bank error.
- Determine whether the bank is considered a debt collector as defined by the FDCPA. If so, ensure appropriate review at the next compliance examination.
- Identify where management has implemented automated decisions (i.e., charge-off, extensions, forbearance) to be consistent with the OCC policy guidelines.

3. Evaluate the adequacy of the bank's classification, nonaccrual, and charge-off practices and whether the practices comply with the bank's written policies and procedures.

- Discuss practices with both management and line personnel. Identify any inconsistencies with policies and procedures versus practices. Ensure examiners assisting with the collection review and conducting testing are aware of these inconsistencies.
- Identify where management has implemented automated processes versus manual processes to comply with policies. Review the system settings to verify that the parameters correspond to those described in the bank's policies and are consistent with FFIEC policies. If not, discuss the differences with management and request appropriate corrective action.
- Request management's summary of classified student loans. Determine if the classification practices are consistent with OCC Bulletin 2000-20. Private student loans should be classified substandard at 90 days past due and loss at 120 days past due.
- Request management's summary of nonaccrual student loans. If the bank does not place student loans on nonaccrual status, determine that the bank employs appropriate

methods to ensure income is accurately measured (e.g., loss allowances for uncollectible fees and finance charges).

- Determine how accounts scheduled for charge-off are loaded into a charge-off queue or other system for loss. Specifically, determine whether losses are automatically or manually processed; what circumstances, if any, will delay a charge-off; and when the bank recognizes losses (i.e., daily, weekly, or monthly).
- Request a report detailing student loans more than 120 days past due that have not been charged off. Review the report with management and determine why those balances remain on the bank's books and whether there are system or policy issues that need to be corrected.

4. Evaluate the adequacy of the bank's policies and practices for payment posting and assessing late fees.

- Review the payment posting procedures and practices and determine if payments are promptly posted.
- Determine the conditions under which late fees are imposed[82] and, if applicable, at what point the fees are suspended.
- Determine the bank's policy for collecting late fees (e.g., as part of the next regularly scheduled payment) and how unpaid late fees are accounted for, tracked, and collected.
- Determine whether the bank's process for evaluating the ramifications of changes in late fee policies, including dollar amounts, is adequate before broad implementation.[83]
- Assess whether the available MIS and reports provide the information necessary to evaluate the effect of late fees. Specifically, assess whether the information is sufficient to allow management to determine whether the fees have the desired effect on performance (i.e., improve on-time payments), whether late fees result in negative amortization, and the extent to which late fees assessed are actually collected.
- Ensure that the bank has established adequate loss allowance for accrued but uncollectible interest and fees, including late fees, in either the allowance or a separate reserve.

5. Assess the appropriateness of management's collection strategies.

- Through discussions with management, determine how management develops collection strategies, who is responsible, and how the success of the strategies is measured.
- Determine what triggers strategy changes and who has authority to direct revisions.
- Establish whether the bank uses scoring or any other predictive techniques to assist in the collection of accounts. If so, determine

---

[82] For example, UDAP concerns could arise from a bank practice of assessing a late fee when the delinquency is only attributable to a late fee assessed on an earlier installment, and the payment is otherwise a full payment for the applicable period and is paid on its due date or within an applicable grace period.

[83] 12 CFR 7.4002(b) sets forth the criteria for national bank fees and charges.

– the scores or techniques used, how they are used, and whether they are internally or externally developed.
– when the scores or techniques were last validated and by whom, and the results of the validation.

6. If applicable, assess the adequacy of the bank's use of collection strategies.

- Identify the person or group responsible for strategy development.
- Determine that the development process begins with a clear identification of strategy objectives and relies on reasonable assumptions and complete and accurate MIS.
- Determine that the bank's controls provide for proper testing of strategies before making decisions to expand penetration.
- Assess the monitoring process and determine whether the bank accumulates and analyzes appropriate data to measure strategy success.
- Determine that the bank maintains adequate documentation of the various strategies.

7. Determine whether the bank uses cure programs such as deferment, extension, forbearance, restructures and modifications, or settlement and forgiveness. If so,

- assess the adequacy of the policies and procedures used to administer the programs and consistency with OCC Bulletin 2000-20, "Uniform Retail Credit Classification and Account Management Policy: Policy Implementation," and CNBE Policy Guidance 2010-2 (REV), "Policy Interpretation: OCC Bulletin 2000-20—Application to Private Student Lending."
- review and evaluate any test and analysis summaries completed before implementation of new cure programs.
- determine whether the bank's programs appropriately address proper income recognition for restructured loans.
- evaluate the MIS and reporting used to monitor and analyze the performance of each program. Compare performance with forecasts, bank objectives, and risk appetite. In addition to reports listed in the bank's collections procedures, ensure that management generates and reviews reports detailing
  – volume (balance and unit) trends for cure program accounts, by product, program, and vintage, and in total.
  – loss performance, by product, program, and vintage, and in total.
  – performance of the accounts 30, 90, 180, 270, 360, etc., days following the cure.
  – performance of accounts cured more than once, broken down by the number of times cured and tracked over time.
  – policy exceptions and the performance of those exceptions.
- compare the performance of accounts in cure programs with the performance of those in the general student loan population using appropriate performance measures.
- assess the current and potential impact of such programs on the bank's reported performance (asset quality) and profitability, including allowance and capital implications.

8. Review and determine the effectiveness of the bank's skip tracing practices and

procedures to track delinquent customers.

- Ascertain what portion of the portfolio lacks current and correct telephone numbers and mailing addresses.
- Evaluate the adequacy of the bank's process for obtaining missing contact information.
- Determine whether the bank has a process to exclude accounts without pertinent contact information from promotional initiatives and favorable account management treatment.
- If applicable, determine whether the bank appropriately monitors outside agencies used to skip-trace accounts.
- Determine whether skip accounts are flagged for accelerated charge-off if attempts to locate the borrower are unsuccessful.

9. Assess whether the bank's automated systems for collecting delinquent accounts are adequate and discuss these systems with management.

- Determine which technologies and processes the bank uses to collect accounts (e.g., automated dialers, collection letters, statement messaging, and e-mail), how each is used, and the key reports generated to monitor performance. Determine whether the reports provide sufficient data to allow management to make appropriate decisions.
- If auto-dialing is used, determine how the system routes "no contact" accounts or accounts that collectors remove from the dialer because of a promise to pay or a payment arrangement.
- Determine whether the systems generate a sufficient audit trail.
- Determine whether managers, supervisors, and quality control staff have the ability to listen to collector phone calls online.
- Evaluate the adequacy of the bank's contingency plans and determine whether the plans are tested regularly.

10. Assess the quality, accuracy, and completeness of MIS reports and other analyses used to manage the collections process.

- Evaluate the quality of MIS collection reports regularly provided to executive management and determine whether the reports provide adequate information, including comparisons with collection objectives and tolerances, for timely decision-making.
- Determine the appropriateness and accuracy of key collection reports. Specifically review
    - vintage and coincident delinquency and loss reports.
    - roll rate reports and migration-to-loss reports.
    - cure program reports, in total, by program and by collector.
    - pipeline reports that track the volume (number and dollar) of accounts entering cure programs, accounts awaiting extension, forbearance, and the actual performance of accounts in the various programs.
    - collector and strategy reports.

– productivity reports, including information such as call frequency, right-party contact, promises made and kept, dollars collected, and staffing summaries.

Note: If not removed, not sufficient funds checks can affect several of the metrics above. Management should have a method to identify, if not correct, the effects of not sufficient funds checks on the metrics.

• Determine whether customer service or a department other than collections can initiate collection activities, such as cure programs. If so, determine whether appropriate MIS are in place to monitor volumes and credit performance of accounts in collection activities initiated outside collections.

11. Determine what system(s) the bank uses to recover charged-off accounts and deficiency balances and whether they interface with the bank's collection management system(s). If not, determine how the recovery unit gathers and uses information about previous collection activities.

12. Determine whether the bank uses outside agencies (including attorneys and attorney networks) to collect delinquent accounts or to recover losses. If so,

• assess the bank's due diligence process for selecting third-party collectors.
• determine whether the bank's legal counsel and compliance officer have reviewed the contracts with and practices of third-party collectors.
• evaluate any forward-flow contracts with collection agencies, including performance tolerances and termination requirements (important for remediation or severing the contract in the event of poor performance). Forward-flow contracts provide agencies with a set number of accounts at a determined frequency and help the bank forecast placements.
• determine the frequency and method of rotating accounts, including reasons supporting the method, between collection and recovery agencies and in-house collections, i.e., distinctions among primary, secondary, and tertiary.
• review productivity and cost reports for each third party, and discuss with management how the bank monitors the success of collectors and allocates workload accordingly.
• evaluate the systems and controls used to supervise out-placed accounts, including active reconcilements of amounts collected and fees disbursed to each third party.
• review MIS used to monitor the performance of outside agencies.
• evaluate the adequacy and frequency of the bank's audits (on-site and remote, if applicable) of third-party collectors.
• determine whether any sales of fully charged-off loans are consistent with OCC Bulletin 2014-37, "Consumer Debt Sales: Risk Management Guidance."

13. Assess the bank's recovery performance using historical results and industry averages, by product, as guidelines.

- Determine whether the bank periodically sells charged-off accounts. If so, determine the reasonableness of forecasts for recoveries.
- Evaluate the bank's recoveries in light of previous period losses.
- Evaluate the accuracy of the recovery figures. If the bank charges accrued but uncollected interest and fees against income rather than the allowance, verify that recoveries are reported accordingly (i.e., include principal only).
- Assess the costs associated with the dollars recovered and explore trends.

14. Assess the appropriateness of the bank's fraud policies and procedures.

- Review the bank's definition of fraud losses and ensure that it is reasonable and appropriately distinguishes fraud from credit losses.
- Ascertain for consistency with the charge-off requirements of OCC Bulletin 2000-20, "Uniform Retail Credit Classification and Account Management Policy: Policy Implementation" (90 days from discovery).
- Confirm that fraud losses are recognized as operating expenses rather than charges to ALLL.

15. Review the adequacy of MIS reports pertaining to fraud.

- Determine whether the information is sufficient to monitor fraud and the effectiveness of fraud controls, including the appropriate filing of suspicious activity reports.
- Assess the levels and trends of fraud losses, by product, compared with industry averages and discuss any atypical findings with management.

16. Assess the adequacy of internal and external audit, quality assurance, loan review, and risk management in the collections area, including scope, frequency, timing, report content, and independence.

- Review relevant audit, quality assurance, loan review, and risk management reports.
- Determine the adequacy and timeliness of management's responses to the issues identified and any findings or issues requiring follow-up. If warranted based on the significance of the issues or concerns about the adequacy of the response or action taken, test corrective action.

17. Conduct transaction testing to verify your initial conclusions on the bank's collection programs and activities. In addition to determining adherence to approved policies and procedures, determine whether the programs and activities result in an enduring positive change in credit risk or provide temporary relief. Verify that MIS reports accurately capture the activities and the subsequent performance of the accounts (refer to appendix A for additional guidance).

- Sample accounts that were at least 60 days delinquent in the month preceding the examination and are now current to determine whether the customer cured the delinquency or whether the account was cured artificially (e.g., extended grace or forbearance). Determine whether the action was consistent with existing bank policy and OCC Bulletin 2000-20, "Uniform Retail Credit Classification and Account Management Policy: Policy Implementation," and CNBE Policy Guidance 2010-2, "Policy Interpretation: OCC Bulletin 2000-20–Application to Private Student Lending."

- Sample accounts from each of the primary collection areas (e.g., early-stage, late-stage, skip, or bankruptcy) to determine adherence to policy. The sample helps an examiner understand the collection process and strategies employed. (**Note:** This sample is often best completed or supplemented by sitting with collectors as they work accounts.)

- Sample loans from each of the following areas to assess compliance with the bank policies for the programs and reasonableness of decisions: recent deferment, extended grace, extension, forbearance, restructures, and modification. Decisions should be compared with the bank's normal underwriting guidelines on amortization period, debt or repayment limitations, and pricing.

- Sample charged-off accounts and review all activities that occurred before charge-off to determine whether the bank employs practices that result in loss deferral.

- Sample identified fraud accounts and review all activities to determine adherence to policy and timeliness of charge-off practices.

18. Develop conclusions regarding the effectiveness of the collection function, including the collection strategies and programs employed, and the implications for the quality of the portfolio and the quantity and direction of credit risk.

Risk Management and Control Functions

Objective: To evaluate the adequacy of the bank's student lending processes for identifying, measuring, monitoring, and controlling risk by reviewing the effectiveness of risk management and other control functions.

1. Assess the structure,[84] management, and staffing of each of the control functions, including risk management, loan review, internal and external audit, quality assurance, and compliance review.

   Note: Compliance is a risk for student lending. While consumer compliance examiners generally assess the quality of the compliance review function, safety and soundness examiners should understand compliance-related roles, responsibilities, and coverage, as well as how compliance controls fit into the overall control plan.

2. Ascertain the roles, responsibilities, and reporting lines of the various control functions through discussions with senior management.

---

[84] Depending on the bank, risk management functions may be managed from different areas in the bank (i.e., some from the line of business and others from the corporate offices).

- Review the organization chart for each function and evaluate the quality and depth of staff (including number of positions) based on the assigned role and the size and complexity of the operation.
  - Review the experience levels of senior managers and staff.
  - Determine whether employees are capable of evaluating the line of business activities.
  - Review management and staff turnover levels.
- Discuss the structure and staffing plans, including known or anticipated gaps or vacancies, with senior management.
- Review compensation plans to determine that performance measurements are appropriately targeted to risk identification and control objectives.
- Determine whether organizational reporting lines create the necessary level of independence.

Note: If the management and staff of a control function lack the knowledge or capability to adequately review all or parts of student lending operations, management may need to consult or hire appropriate outside expertise.

3. Discuss with senior managers how they assess whether significant risks are appropriately monitored by at least one control function and how they assess the effectiveness of each function.

4. Determine whether the risk management function appropriately monitors, analyzes, and controls the bank's credit risk.

- Determine risk management's recurring responsibilities and major projects, including status of projects, and assess the adequacy of those activities in light of the bank's student lending risk profile, the products offered, and the complexity of the operation.
- Determine whether credit risk decisions involve all key functional areas, including risk management, marketing, finance, operations, compliance, legal, and information technology, either formally or informally.
- Determine whether risk management is involved in tactical student lending decisions, such as program approvals, program renewals, new products, marketing campaigns, and annual financial planning.
- Obtain descriptions of key management reports to determine the types and purposes of reports produced, report distribution, and frequency of preparation.
- Obtain a sample of recent ad hoc or special studies or board reports produced by risk management to determine the types of analyses performed, the reasonableness of the scopes and methodologies used, and the accuracy of the conclusions drawn, including the adequacy of the support provided.
- Determine what technologies and risk tools are deployed and risk management's role in the management of those tools, including data warehouse, portfolio management software, credit scoring, and risk models.
- Determine whether market, competitive, legislative, and other external factors are considered in the risk management process.

5. Determine whether management considers consumer complaints and complaint resolution in the risk management process. Obtain copies of complaints filed with the OCC (complaints reported to the Customer Assistance Group) and the CFPB (using the Consumer Complaint Database), and bank consumer complaint logs and evaluate the information for significant issues and trends. Complaints often serve as a valuable early warning indicator for compliance, credit, and operational issues, including discriminatory, unfair, deceptive, abusive, and predatory practices.

6. Determine whether changes to practices and products, including new products and practices, are fully tested, analyzed, and supported before broad implementation.

7. Test the effectiveness of the bank's risk management process for existing and new products, marketing and collection initiatives, and changes to risk appetite (e.g., initiating or changing credit criteria or adopting new scoring systems and technologies). Select at least one significant new product or collections initiative (e.g., forbearance or modification), and track it through all facets of the management process.

    - **Planning:** If tracking a new loan product, for example, determine how the bank developed new underwriting standards (e.g., how did it analyze the applicability of the underwriting criteria and marketing strategies then in use and what was the basis of any projections?), and how did it derive new criteria or strategies (e.g., what were the key drivers for credit and revenue?).
    - **Execution:** Evaluate the adequacy of the process employed to ensure that new criteria and changes were implemented as intended. This component is generally performed by some combination of information technology staff, product management, quality control, audit, and loan operations.
    - **Measurement:** Ascertain how adherence to standards is measured and how management measures affect using back-end monitoring and analysis. Determine the key measurements management uses to analyze the effectiveness of its decisions (e.g., responder analyses, first or early payment default, vintage reporting for delinquencies and losses, risk-adjusted margin, and profit and loss) and the adequacy of back-testing analyses (comparison to targets, identification and analysis of anomalies).
    - **Adjustment:** Determine how feedback results (lessons learned, opportunities identified) are incorporated into the process as course corrections or adjustments. Assess the process for making adjustments as problems or unexpected performance results are identified, and whether the process is both timely and appropriate.

8. Determine whether the bank has the data warehousing capabilities (i.e., the capacity to store and retrieve pertinent data) to support necessary monitoring, analytical, and forecasting activities.

9. Evaluate executive management's monthly and quarterly report packages. Specifically,

    - determine whether the reports accurately and completely describe the state of the bank's student lending business.

- evaluate whether reports adequately measure credit risk (e.g., score distributions and vintage reports), identify trends, describe significant variances, and present issues. (**Note:** Reports should allow management to assess whether student lending operations remain consistent with strategic objectives and within established risk, return, and credit performance tolerances.)
- determine whether reports clearly indicate analysis of performance results and trends rather than merely depict data.

10. Obtain feedback from other examiners assigned to the student lending examination regarding the adequacy of reports available.

Credit Scoring Models

Note: Refer to OCC Bulletins 1997-24, "Credit Scoring Models: Examiner Guidance," and 2011-12, "Supervisory Guidance on Model Risk Management," for additional background and guidance in this area.

11. Assess the adequacy of the student loan scorecard management process, and determine the effectiveness of the department or personnel responsible for scorecard and model development or procurement, implementation (including monitoring), and validation.

- Obtain a model inventory to determine the models in use. The inventory should include
  - name of the model.
  - model description.
  - type (custom, generic, behavioral).
  - date developed.
  - source (name of the third-party or in-house modeler).
  - purpose (e.g., pricing, profitability, or collectability).
  - date last validated and next scheduled validation date.
  - model rating from either the last validation or ongoing monitoring.
  - models under development, if any.
  - management contact for each model.
- Determine whether scorecards are used for purposes consistent with the development process and populations. If not (e.g., applied to a different product or new geographic area), assess the ramifications and acceptability.
- Review the most recent independent validation reports for key risk models and discuss the conclusions with risk management.
- Discuss how management uses the models to target prospects, underwrite applications, and manage the portfolio.
- Determine how management measures the ongoing performance and robustness of models (e.g., good and bad separation, bad rate analysis, and maximum delinquency ["ever bad"] distribution reports).
- Review scorecard tracking reports to determine how well the models are performing. Select tracking reports for key models and determine whether model performance is stable or deteriorating, and how management compensates for deteriorating efficacy.

- Determine how cutoffs are established, reviewed, and adjusted. Review the most recent cutoff analysis for key risk models.
- Determine the bank's score override policy, assess the adequacy of associated tracking, and review override volume and performance. Determine whether management segments low-side overrides by reason and tracks delinquencies or defaults by reason and override score bands, and assess the performance and trends.
- Review chronology logs to determine changes in the credit criteria or risk profile and to explain shifts in the portfolio, including volume and performance.

12. Select at least one key student loan credit risk scoring model and fully assess the adequacy of the model management process.

- Review the original model documentation or scorecard manual, and assess management's adherence to the modeler's recommended scorecard maintenance routine.
- Compare the population characteristics and the developmental sample performance by log odds ratio with the bank's current experience.
- Review model performance reports and assess the adequacy of management's response to the issues or trends identified. Reports reviewed may include applicant distribution, population stability, characteristic analysis (if indicated by a population shift), override tracking, and vintage delinquency and loss distribution reports.

Loan Review

13. Assess the adequacy of the loan review process for student lending. Determine whether

- the loan review's scope includes providing a risk assessment of the quality of risk management and quantity of risk for student lending in aggregate and by student loan program.
- the scope includes appropriate testing for adherence to key credit policies and procedures.
- the scope includes appropriate reviews to assess compliance with applicable laws, regulations, and consistency with regulatory guidance.
- the scope includes a review of the accuracy and adequacy of MIS reporting.
- the frequency of reviews is acceptable based on the significance of the risks involved.
- staffing levels and experience are commensurate with the complexity and risk in the student lending area.
- loan review is independent from the production process.
- loan review possesses sufficient authority and influence to correct deficiencies or curb dangerous practices.

14. Evaluate recent loan review reports for student lending. Determine whether

- reports are issued in a timely manner following completion of the on-site work.
- reports provide meaningful conclusions and accurately identify concerns.

- significant issues require management's written response.
- management initiates timely and appropriate corrective action.
- issues identified and the status of corrective actions are tracked and reported to senior management.

Note: Weaknesses identified by examiners, but not identified by the loan review, may be evidence of deficiencies in loan review processes or staffing.

Quality Control

15. Assess the adequacy of the quality control process for student lending. Determine whether

- the process assesses ongoing compliance with key credit and operational policies and procedures, and applicable laws and regulations for all primary areas, including
    - loan origination.
    - account management.
    - customer service.
    - collections.

    Note: Quality control processes should be established for all student lending activities and any third-party loan servicing and origination arrangements.

- quality control tests the integrity and accuracy of MIS data for areas listed above.
- the frequency of reviews is properly geared to the significance of the risk.
- the testing and sample sizes are appropriate.
- the quality control function possesses sufficient authority and influence to correct deficiencies or curb dangerous practices.

16. Review a sample of quality assurance ongoing testing worksheets and periodic summary reports (e.g., monthly summaries of testing conclusions). Determine whether

- the reporting process allows for timely feedback to management.
- worksheets and summary reports accurately identify concerns.
- significant issues require management's written response.
- management initiates timely and appropriate corrective action.
- issues identified and the status of corrective actions are tracked and reported to senior management.

Note: Weaknesses identified by examiners, but not identified by the quality control function, may be evidence of deficiencies in quality control processes or staffing.

17. If the quality assurance function is not independent from the loan production process, determine whether internal audit or loan review tests quality assurance to ensure that management can rely on those findings.

18. If reviews and testing by the quality control area do not include significant risk areas, communicate findings to the EIC to determine whether it is appropriate to complete transactional testing in areas not covered by quality control.

Internal Audit

19. Assess the adequacy of internal audit for student lending. Determine whether

   - the scope includes appropriate testing for adherence to key credit and operational policies and procedures.
   - the frequency of reviews is properly geared to the significance of the risks.
   - internal audit is independent.
   - internal audit possesses sufficient authority and influence to correct deficiencies or curb dangerous practices.

   Note: Refer to the "Internal and External Audits" booklet of the *Comptroller's Handbook* for additional information.

20. Review recent internal audit reports for student lending. Determine whether

   - reports are issued in a timely manner following completion of the on-site work.
   - reports accurately identify concerns.
   - significant issues require management's written response.
   - management initiates timely and appropriate corrective action.
   - issues identified and the status of corrective actions are tracked and reported to senior management.

   Note: Weaknesses identified by examiners, but not identified by internal audit, may be evidence of deficiencies in internal audit processes or staffing.

Other Controls

21. Confirm that there is an adequate student lending process in place to reconcile major balance sheet categories and general ledger entries on a daily basis.

22. Identify and determine the adequacy of the bank's student lending process for regularly evaluating data integrity and MIS accuracy.

   - Review the scope and frequency of internal audit or other reviews of MIS accuracy.
   - Review the findings of the most recent reviews.

23. Develop conclusions on the adequacy of the bank's processes for identifying, measuring, monitoring, and controlling risk by reviewing the effectiveness of risk management and other control functions. Clearly document all findings.

Profitability

Objective: To assess the quantity, quality, and sustainability of student lending earnings.

> **Note:** For banks that securitize, examiners should review income statements for managed assets.

1. Obtain and review copies of the income statement for the student loan portfolio and for each significant form of student loan offered. Assess whether the reports include all pertinent income and expense items including overhead and funding costs.

2. Ascertain the contribution of the student loan portfolio to earnings and the expected contribution in the future.

    - Review executive management monthly or quarterly performance reports and portfolio quality MIS packages.
    - Review historical trends, including changes in the product contributions.
    - Review financial projections and budget and plan variances.
    - Review significant income and expense components and measures. Items reviewed should include noninterest income (fees and other add-ons), marketing expenses, charge-offs, net interest margin, and risk-adjusted yield.
    - Evaluate the methodologies, assumptions, and documentary support for the bank's planning and forecasting processes. Determine whether material changes are expected in any of the key income and expense components and measures.
    - Determine the bank's return on assets[85] and return on equity[86] hurdles, and the actual returns as of the examination date. Asset-based measures are typically more meaningful for comparison because banks allocate capital differently.

3. Verify that the bank appropriately recognizes uncollectible accrued interest and fees through ALLL, through a separate interest and fee reserve, or through cash income recognition.

4. Review the bank's stress test and discuss potential earnings volatility through an economic cycle with management to assess sustainability. If the bank does not perform stress testing, discuss if and how management prices loans to withstand economic downturns.

5. Determine whether the bank's cost accounting system is capable of generating profit data by product, segment (including grade), channel, and account.

---

[85] The bank's return on assets is an indicator of how profitable the bank is relative to its total assets and can show how efficiently management uses its assets to generate earnings. Return on assets is calculated by dividing a bank's annual earnings by its total assets.

[86] Return on equity means the amount of net income returned as a percentage of shareholders' equity.

6. Assess the profitability of each product.

   - For each product, review profitability by credit score band, credit grade, sub-portfolio, school, and vintage, as appropriate.
   - Compare actual results with projections and discuss variances with management.

7. Evaluate profitability by channel.

   - Through discussions with the examiner responsible for third-party management, determine profitability generated through the various channels (e.g., third-party originators).
   - Compare the profitability of the loans generated by the various channels.

8. Determine the adequacy of the pricing method.

   - Review the pricing strategy, pricing method, and pricing model, if applicable.
   - Review the major assumptions used in the pricing method and assess reasonableness. Be alert to differences in assumptions by product and channel.
   - Determine whether pricing is driven by risk, capital, or some other allocation method or hurdle, and how much, if any, it is driven by the competition.
   - Determine whether the pricing method incorporates a realistic break-even analysis, and whether the analysis reflects the true costs of prolonged deferment of student loans and default rates of certain student loan programs.
   - Review the pricing matrix, by product.

9. Assess the adequacy of planning, reporting, and analysis with respect to deferment. Specifically, ascertain whether management identifies the volume and trends of student loans with high default rates relative to market to determine exposure and impact on earnings.

10. Develop conclusions on the quantity, quality, and sustainability of earnings.

Third-Party Relationship Risk Management

Objective: To determine the extent of third-party involvement in student lending activities and evaluate the effectiveness of management's third-party oversight and risk management processes.

These procedures apply to any arrangements with third parties to provide student loan-related services to customers on the bank's behalf. Banks may fully "outsource" loan originations, servicing, collection activities (using collection agencies or attorneys), or the offering of products in the bank's name.

Refer to OCC Bulletin 2013-29, "Third-Party Relationships: Risk Management Guidance," for additional information on OCC expectations.

1. Determine the adequacy of the bank's third-party risk management program.

   - Assess the adequacy of the risk management policy and determine that analysis, documentation, and reporting requirements are clearly addressed.
   - Determine that management has designated an individual to be responsible for the program and has delegated the authority necessary for its effective administration to that individual.
   - Review the bank's process for maintaining a complete list of third parties used by the bank.
   - Review the bank's criteria for designating "significant" third parties according to the dollar amount of the contract, the importance of the service provided, and the potential risk involved in the activity. While the risk management program should address all third-party relationships, the OCC expects a more rigorous process to manage those third parties deemed significant.
   - Review the bank's due diligence process and determine whether the process
     - provides for comprehensive, well-documented reviews by qualified staff.
     - identifies any potential conflicts of interest with bank directors, officers, staff, and their related interests.
     - addresses compliance with all applicable laws and regulations, including safety and soundness regulatory standards, and laws prohibiting lending discrimination and unfair or deceptive practices.

2. Identify third parties that provide significant student loan services on the bank's behalf, particularly those that provide loan origination and servicing of both private and FFELP runoff portfolios. Determine the bank's relationship manager for each of those third parties.

3. Verify that bank management's expertise in the outsourced activities is sufficient to accurately identify and manage the risks involved.

4. Determine whether management has adequate controls, including policies, procedures and monitoring controls, to avoid becoming involved with a third party engaged in discriminatory, unfair, deceptive, abusive, or predatory lending practices. If weaknesses or concerns are found, consult the bank's EIC or compliance examiner.

   Note: For additional information, refer to the "Fair Lending" booklet of the *Comptroller's Handbook* and OCC Advisory Letter 2002-3, "Guidance on Unfair or Deceptive Acts or Practices."

5. Assess the adequacy of contract management, focusing on the process for ensuring that clauses necessary to effectively manage the third parties are included.

   - Determine whether the bank has a current contract on file for all third parties and that the bank monitors key dates (e.g., maturity, renewal, and adjustment periods).
   - Review a sample of contracts with significant third parties to confirm that the contracts satisfactorily address the following:

- Scope of the arrangement, including the frequency, content, and format of services provided by each party.
- Outsourcing notifications or approvals required, if the third party proposes to subcontract a service to another party.
- All costs and compensation, including any incentives.
- Performance standards, including when standards can be adjusted and the consequences of failing to meet those standards.
- Reporting and MIS requirements.
- Data ownership and access.
- Appropriate privacy and confidentiality restrictions.
- Requirements for compliance with all applicable laws and regulations, including safety and soundness regulatory standards, and laws prohibiting lending discrimination and unfair or deceptive practices.
- Mandatory third-party control functions such as quality assurance and audit, including requirements for submitting audit results to the bank.
- Expectations and responsibilities for business resumption and contingency plans.
- Responsibility for consumer complaint resolution and associated reporting to the bank.
- Third-party financial statement submission requirements.
- Appropriate dispute resolution, liability, recourse, penalty, indemnification, and termination clauses.
- The authority for the bank to perform on-site third-party reviews. Third-party performance of services is subject to OCC examination oversight.

- Determine whether the bank's monitoring of third parties' adherence to the bank's contracts (especially to financial terms and performance standards) is adequate in frequency and scope.
- Determine whether issues identified through the monitoring process are appropriately resolved in a timely manner.

6. Assess the adequacy of the monitoring process for significant third parties.

- Using the sample of significant third parties reviewed in the previous procedure, confirm that the bank's oversight incorporates, at a minimum,
  - reports evidencing the third party's performance relative to service-level agreements and other contract provisions.
  - customer complaints and resolutions for the services and products outsourced.
  - third-party financial statements and audit reports.
  - compliance with applicable laws and regulations.
- Evaluate whether the process results in an accurate determination of whether contractual terms and conditions are being met, and whether any revisions to service-level agreements or other terms are needed.
- Verify whether management documents and follows up on performance, operational, or compliance problems and whether the documentation and follow-ups are timely and effective.
- Determine whether the relationship manager or other bank staff periodically meets with its third parties to discuss performance and operational issues.

- Determine whether third-party risk management administers call monitoring, mystery shopper, customer callback, or customer satisfaction programs, if appropriate.
- Assess the adequacy of the bank's process for determining when on-site reviews are warranted, the scope of those reviews, and reporting of results.
- Determine whether management evaluates the third party's ongoing ability to perform the contracted functions in a satisfactory manner based on performance and financial condition.

7. For third-party loan originators,

- assess the adequacy of the process used to qualify third parties for loan origination.
- assess the adequacy of the reports and tracking mechanisms in place to monitor performance (e.g., volume of applications submitted, approved, and booked; quality; exceptions; and loan performance) and relationship profitability, including performance and profitability compared with projections.
- assess the adequacy of the process used to monitor compliance with the bank's lending policies, and applicable laws and regulations.
- verify that management maintains a watch list for problematic originators and that actions taken (including termination of the relationship, if warranted) are appropriate and timely.

8. Assess the adequacy of the content, accuracy, and distribution of third-party management program reports.

9. Determine whether the bank has any loans to the third party and whether any other conflicts of interest exist.

10. Determine whether any insiders have relationships with the third parties used by the bank and whether any potential conflicts of interest exist (e.g., insider has ownership interests, officer or board positions, or loans to the third party).

11. Determine whether the bank is involved in any significant third-party relationships where deficiencies in management expertise or controls result in the failure to adequately identify and manage the associated risk. If so, consult with the EIC and the supervisory office and determine whether it is appropriate to require that the activity be suspended pending satisfactory corrective action.

12. Develop conclusions on the extent of third-party involvement in student lending activities and the effectiveness of management's third-party oversight and risk management processes. Include any Education Department servicer review findings. Clearly document all findings.

Conclusions

Conclusion: The aggregate level of each associated risk is (low, moderate, or high). The direction of each associated risk is (increasing, stable, or decreasing).

Objective: To determine, document, and communicate overall findings and conclusions regarding the examination of student lending.

1. Determine preliminary examination findings and conclusions and discuss with the EIC, including

   - quantity of associated risks (as noted in the "Introduction" section).
   - quality of risk management.
   - aggregate level and direction of associated risks.
   - overall risk in student lending.
   - violations and other concerns.

Summary of Risks Associated With Student Lending				
Risk category	Quantity of risk (Low, moderate, high)	Quality of risk management (Weak, insufficient, satisfactory, strong)	Aggregate level of risk (Low, moderate, high)	Direction of risk (Increasing, stable, decreasing)
Credit				
Interest rate				
Liquidity				
Operational				
Compliance				
Strategic				
Reputation				

2. If substantive safety and soundness concerns remain unresolved that may have a material adverse effect on the bank, further expand the scope of the examination by completing verification procedures.

3. Discuss examination findings with bank management, including violations, recommendations, and conclusions about risks and risk management practices. If necessary, obtain commitments for corrective action.

4. Compose conclusion comments, highlighting any issues that should be included in the ROE. If necessary, compose a matters requiring attention comment.

5. Update the OCC's information system and any applicable ROE schedules or tables.

6. Write a memorandum specifically setting out what the OCC should do in the future to effectively supervise student lending in the bank, including time periods, staffing, and workdays required.

7. Update, organize, and reference work papers in accordance with OCC policy.

8. Ensure any paper or electronic media that contain sensitive bank or customer information are appropriately disposed of or secured.

Internal Control Questionnaire

An ICQ helps an examiner assess a bank's internal controls for an area. ICQs typically address standard controls that provide day-to-day protection of bank assets and financial records. The examiner decides the extent to which it is necessary to complete or update ICQs during examination planning or after reviewing the findings and conclusions of the core assessment.

Policies

1. Has the board of directors, consistent with its duties and responsibilities, adopted written policies that established

   - procedures for reviewing student loan applications?
   - standards for determining loan amounts?
   - minimum standards for documentation?
   - standards for collection procedures?

2. Are policies reviewed at least annually to determine that they are compatible with changing market conditions, the bank's risk profile, and the bank's strategic plan?

Underwriting and Scoring Models

3. Does audit or internal loan review test compliance with student loan underwriting standards?

4. Are underwriting standards periodically reviewed and revised?

5. If credit scoring models are used,

   - are credit limits determined by cutoff scores?
   - are models periodically revalidated?
   - are there internal procedures governing overrides?

6. Is data from the application tested for input accuracy to the bank's account processing system? If so, what is the sample size and frequency of the test?

7. Is an exception report produced and reviewed by management that includes student loan deferment, extensions, forbearance, restructure, modification, or other factors that would result in a change in customer account status?

8. Does the student lending operation prepare a budget by

   - function (e.g., collections or application processing)?
   - program (e.g., graduate, undergraduate, or profession)?

- overall line of business?

9. Are actual results compared to budget at least monthly?

10. Are significant trends and deviations adequately explained in the financial review process?

11. Do asset securitizations receive appropriate approval?

12. Are collection programs for securitized loans appropriate?

13. Does management have a plan to ensure adequate funding for maturing securitizations?

Risk Management

14. Does management develop and maintain student lending underwriting and account management guidelines?

15. Does management monitor adherence to those guidelines?

16. Does management ascertain the quality of the portfolio and assign risk ratings?

17. Does management periodically review policies and procedures for adequacy and assess their impact on portfolio quality?

18. Does management adequately assess the integrity of scoring systems and other models in use?

Conclusion

19. Is the foregoing information an adequate basis for evaluating internal controls in that there are no significant additional internal auditing procedures, accounting controls, administrative controls, or other circumstances that impair any controls or mitigate any weaknesses indicated above? (Explain negative answers briefly and indicate conclusions as to their effect on specific examination or verification procedures).

20. Based on the answers to the foregoing questions, internal control for student lending is considered (strong, satisfactory, insufficient, or weak).

Verification Procedures

Verification procedures are used to verify the existence of assets and liabilities, or test the reliability of financial records. Examiners generally do not perform verification procedures as part of a typical examination. Rather, verification procedures are performed when substantive safety and soundness concerns are identified that are not mitigated by the bank's risk management systems and internal controls.

Objective: To verify the authenticity of the bank's student loans and test the accuracy of records and adequacy of record keeping.

Note: Examiners normally do not need to perform extensive verification. These procedures, however, are appropriate when the bank has inadequate audit coverage of student lending activities or when fraud or other irregularities are suspected.

1. Test the additions of the trial balances and the reconciliation of the trial balances to the general ledger. Include loan commitments and other contingent liabilities.

2. After selecting loans from the trial balance by using an appropriate sampling technique (refer to the "Sampling Methodologies" booklet of the *Comptroller's Handbook* for guidance on sampling techniques),

    *   prepare and mail confirmation forms to borrowers. (Loans serviced by other institutions, either whole loans or participations, are usually confirmed only with the servicing institution. Loans serviced for other institutions, either whole loans or participations, should be confirmed with the buying institution and the borrower. Confirmation forms should include borrower's name, loan number, the original amount, interest rate, current loan balance, and borrower status).
    *   after a reasonable time, mail second requests.
    *   follow up on any unanswered requests for verification or exceptions and resolve differences.
    *   examine notes for completeness and compare agree date, amount, and terms with trial balance.
    *   in the event notes are not held at the bank, request confirmation by the holder.
    *   check to see that required officer approvals are on the note.
    *   check to see that note is signed, appears to be genuine, and is negotiable.

3. Review accounts with accrued interest by

    *   reviewing and testing procedures for accounting for accrued interest and for handling adjustments.
    *   scanning accrued interest for any unusual entries and following up on any unusual items by tracing them to initial and supporting records.

4. Using a list of nonaccruing loans, check loan accrual records to determine that interest income is not being recorded.

5. Obtain or prepare a schedule showing the monthly interest income amounts and the loan balance at each month's end since the last examination, and

- calculate yield.
- investigate any significant fluctuations or trends.

Appendixes

Appendix A: Transaction Testing

Overview

Examiners should perform testing procedures when the EIC determines that the OCC should verify a bank's compliance with its own policies and procedures or with regulatory policies, regulations, or laws. The EIC institutes testing when deemed appropriate to assess the bank's risk selection, the accuracy of the bank's MIS, or the accuracy of its loan accounting and servicing. Testing procedures usually are performed periodically on student loan portfolios or targeted segments of the portfolios, and when there is elevated risk (e.g., loans to students attending for-profit schools), an increase in delinquency and loss rates, new student loan programs, new acquisition channels, or rapid growth, or when loan review or audit is inadequate.

Examiners conducting testing should be alert for potential discriminatory, unfair, deceptive, abusive, or predatory lending practices (e.g., providing misleading disclosures). If weaknesses are found or other concerns arise, consult the bank's EIC or compliance examiner.

These procedures recommend judgmental sample sizes. Sample sizes are suggestions only. The sample size and targeted portfolio segment may be modified to fit the circumstances. The sample selected should be sufficient in size to reach a supportable conclusion. Increase the sample size if questions arise and more evidence is needed to support the conclusion.

Examiners may want to consider using a statistical sampling process for reaching conclusions on an entire portfolio. Performing statistically valid transaction testing on portfolios of homogeneous retail accounts is extremely effective. The benefits of statistical sampling allow the examiner to quantify the results of transaction testing and state with a statistically valid level of confidence that the results are reliable. For additional information, consult the "Sampling Methodologies" booklet of the *Comptroller's Handbook*.

Note: Appropriate sample size may vary based on the volume and complexity of the bank's private student lending activities.

Underwriting

Objective: To determine the quality of new student loans and risk selection. Determine adherence to lending policy, underwriting standards, and pricing standards.

Sample size—30	Loans and accounts booked in the last 90 days.
	• Include coverage of all significant student loan products.
	• Include all or target certain acquisition channels.
	• Include different price points.

Sample size—10 from third-party origination channel	Loans and accounts approved and booked in the last 90 days.
	• Include all significant third-party loan originators.

Sample size—30	Loans and accounts declined in the last 90 days.
	• Include coverage of all significant student loan products.
	• Include all or target certain acquisition channels.
	• Focus on applications not automatically denied if credit scoring is used.

Lending Policy Exceptions

Objective: To evaluate the quality and appropriateness of exceptions to lending policy.

Sample size—30	Loan and accounts booked in the last 90 days.
	• Include all exception codes.
	• Include coverage of all significant product types.
	• Include loans with exceptions from all significant third-party loan originators (if any).
	• If exception coding is deficient, filter new loans for exceptions to debt-to-income, credit history, etc., and select sample.

Overrides

Objective: To evaluate the quality and appropriateness of low-score overrides.

Sample size—30	Loan and accounts booked in the last 90 days.
	• Select loans that scored below cutoff and were approved.
	• Include all score override reason codes.
	• Include loans in all score bands below the cutoff.

Collection Activities

Objective: To evaluate appropriateness of collection activities and consistency with OCC Bulletin 2000-20, "Uniform Retail Credit Classification and Account Management Policy: Policy Implementation," and CNBE Policy Guidance 2010-2 (REV), "Policy Interpretation: OCC Bulletin 2000-20—Application to Private Student Lending." **Note:** Refer to the checklist in appendix C of this booklet.

Payment Extensions

Sample size—30	Student loans that received extended grace periods in the past three months that brought the loans to current status.
	• Include loans that were two payments or more past due.
	• Check consistency with FFIEC policies.
	• Check compliance with bank policies.

Restructures and Modifications

Sample size—30	Student loans that were restructured and modified in the past three months. <ul><li>Check consistency with FFIEC policies.</li><li>Check compliance with bank policies.</li></ul>

Forbearance, Extension, and Workout Programs

Sample size—30 per program	Student loans that were in a workout program in the past three months. <ul><li>Include any program with payment amount, interest, or fee modification.</li><li>Verify how the minimum payment is calculated.</li><li>Select 50 percent of sample from accounts that entered the program in the last quarter.</li><li>Evaluate the reasonableness of programs, i.e., qualifying criteria, interest rate, payment amount, and repayment period.</li><li>Verify compliance with internal policies and procedures.</li><li>Determine the type and length of time in temporary hardship program.</li><li>Be alert to the movement of accounts from one program to another or stacking of workout arrangements.</li></ul>

Settlement

Sample size—30	Student loans with settlement agreements in the past three months. <ul><li>Verify compliance with internal policies and procedures.</li><li>Evaluate the reasonableness of the repayment period.</li><li>Determine the appropriateness of loan allowance and charge-offs.</li></ul>

Was Past Due, Now Current

Sample size—30	Student loans that were 90 days or more past due as of three months ago but current as of the next month. <ul><li>Check consistency with FFIEC policies.</li><li>Check compliance with bank policies.</li><li>Determine how the loan returned to current status and its appropriateness.</li><li>Assess the accuracy of the loan accounting system and delinquency reporting.</li><li>Consider the impact of any irregularities on roll rates and loan loss method.</li></ul>

Sample size—30	Student loans that were 60 days or more past due as of three months ago but are current in the next month. <ul><li>Check consistency with FFIEC policies.</li><li>Check compliance with bank policies.</li><li>Determine how the loan returned to current status and its appropriateness.</li><li>Assess the accuracy of the loan accounting system and delinquency reporting.</li><li>Consider the impact of any irregularities on roll rates and loan loss method.</li></ul>

Exceptions to Charge-Off Policy

Sample size—30	Student loans more than 120 days past due as of examination date.
	• Include loans from each product type.
	• Check consistency with FFIEC policies.
	• Check compliance with bank policies.
	• Evaluate whether exceptions to FFIEC policy are appropriate.

Charge-Off Post Mortem

Sample size—30	Recently charged-off loans.
	• Include loans from each product type.
	• Check consistency with FFIEC policies.
	• Check compliance with bank policies.
	• Review borrower, payment, and collection histories to determine whether actions taken pre-charge-off were reasonable or if the practices deferred loss recognition.
	• Evaluate whether exceptions to FFIEC policy are appropriate.

Appendix B: Sample Request Letter

Provide the following information for student lending operations as of the close of business [DATE], unless otherwise indicated. Information in an electronic format is preferred. If submitting hard copies, prominently mark any information and documentation that is to be returned to the bank.

Our intent is to request information that can be easily obtained. If you find that the information and documentation are not readily available or require significant effort on your part to compile, contact us before compiling the data.

Note that the following list is not all-inclusive. We may request additional items during the course of our on-site examination, as well as thereafter.

General

1. Summary of each student loan product offered and a brief description of characteristics and terms. Include marketing or acquisition channels used (e.g., direct, Internet, mail, and third-party originators), where applicable.

2. Descriptions of any new or expanded products or marketing initiatives since the last examination and any upcoming plans, including information on criteria and eligibility.

3. Descriptions of any third-party loan generation or servicing arrangements (e.g., collection agencies).

4. Descriptions of any student loan portfolios acquired since the last examination, including due diligence reports.

Senior Management and Oversight

5. For any senior management and oversight committees, the most current committee management information system (MIS) package and the last 12 months of committee minutes.

6. Current set of organizational charts for all functions, including supporting necessary operations. Provide contact information for all key managers.

7. If available, a current version of the student lending strategic plan. At a minimum, we would like to arrange for a meeting to discuss the major strategic initiatives and assumptions involved in this process.

8. Current income statement and balance sheet that compare actual results against the original and updated forecast. If available, provide product level profitability information.

9. Any updated competitive market analysis, industry trade publications, or economic data that management reviews on a regular basis.

10. Any additional key MIS reports that are not provided elsewhere and that are used by senior management to oversee the student lending unit.

Underwriting

11. Chronological log of policy or credit criteria changes implemented since the last examination, along with a listing of other significant changes to operating procedures. Provide available approval decks.

12. Summary reports of [DATE] and year-to-date [DATE] application volume, including approvals, denials, and withdrawals by product and channel.

13. Description of loan policy exception tracking systems, along with the most recent summary reports of underwriting exceptions. Describe monitoring and control processes.

14. Current copies of matrices or tables detailing the underwriting process.

15. Policy guidelines for new products or major modification to an existing product, e.g., planning, testing, roll-out, monitoring, and pro forma review.

16. Criteria for the cosigner release option. Provide information on the number of borrowers (and percent of borrowers in repayment) who qualified for this program during [DATE] and year-to-date [DATE] and any performance tracking of this program (on-time payment qualifiers).

Risk Management

17. Complete set of current risk management reports utilized to assess the quality of borrowers and monitor portfolio risk.

18. All risk management executive summary reports created for [DATE] and year-to-date [DATE] that address growth, delinquencies, losses, bankruptcies, portfolio composition, and other portfolio data.

19. Current [DATE] growth and loss forecasts for each major portfolio segment.

20. Summary monthly delinquency and net loss reports for each portfolio, including the most recent vintage and loss analysis, along with current delinquency and loss distributions by key credit characteristics.

21. Information on performance and loss assumptions for private student loan portfolios originated under third-party underwriting guidelines.

22. Narrative description of any account management practices employed by the bank.

23. List of all models used for origination and pricing including model name, purpose and use, developer, date implemented, date last validated, model rating, and a contact name for questions. Ensure this list includes

    - any model used to determine the approved list of schools.
    - any validation and subsequent revision in the weighting of attributes used in existing models.

24. Description of the bank's concentration limits by key portfolio segments. Explain how these limits are determined and monitored.

25. Description of the methodology used to forecast losses and how the bank accounts for different external and internal factors. Indicate how this information is used in the quarterly ALLL analysis.

26. Results of any stress testing exercise, along with supporting documentation that explains the scenarios considered and key assumptions involved in the process. Identify any actions taken by management in response to the test results.

School Relationship Management

27. Current listing of approved educational institutions. Include number and volume of [DATE] originations for the top 50 institutions as defined by number of accounts.

28. Reports used by management to monitor application volume and loan quality by individual institution.

29. Written criteria for approving new institutions, along with guidelines for monitoring institution relationships. Include information on grading systems, if applicable.

30. Management's most recent analysis of school criteria and justification for continuing to accept business with institutions that exceed the maximum educational institution parameters.

31. Listing of schools where [BANK] allows an exception to the annual per student lending limit, and the current limit for each of these schools.

Collections

32. Detailed roll rate reports for the portfolio and each major segment.

33. Internal guidelines and policies for charge-offs, deferments, extensions, payment modification, settlement, and any other forbearance programs currently in effect or used during the previous 12 months. Provide summary MIS and trend analysis for each.

34. Description of process used to identify accounts with forbearance (including multiple forbearance instances) and to ensure that bank forbearance policies are being adhered to. Provide summary MIS.

35. Delinquency and loss information on forbearance accounts.

36. Full description of charge-off exception programs and relevant MIS reports. Provide the approval authority matrix for each program. Include lists of all accounts excepted from charge-off during [DATE].

37. List of accounts that were 90 or more days past due on [DATE] and current (less than 30 days past due) on [DATE]. Include name, account number, balance, date of last payment, amount of last payment, next due date, next payment amount due, and delinquency stage on each respective date, and any identifying character showing whether the account is in a deferment or forbearance program.

38. Description of collection or behavior scoring models used in collection processes.

39. Any analysis conducted on early payment defaults during [DATE].

40. Collection policies and procedures.

Marketing

41. Information for any significant marketing initiatives planned for [DATE].

Information Technology

42. Current list of primary applications and systems, including location and third party.

Quality Assurance, External and Internal Audits

43. The [DATE] quality assurance testing plan, along with a listing of tests completed over the past [NUMBER OF] months.

44. Summary of significant findings resulting from quality assurance reviews conducted over the past six months. Provide management's response and current status of any outstanding issues.

45. Copies of recent external audits, including those performed by the Education Department and the external auditor for government-insured loans and management's responses to these audits.

46. Copies of recent internal audits, including current status reports concerning corrective action taken to address issues identified in internal audit reports issued since [DATE].

Third-Party Relationship Risk Management

47. Listing of all third parties used by the bank in relation to private student loan offerings along with a description of the services provided, type of relationship, role in the product cycle or channel, and any cost or compensation program in [DATE] and year-to-date [DATE].

Allowance for Loan and Lease Losses

48. Most recent ALLL analysis for the student lending portfolio. Include a complete description of the method and assumptions used.

Other Areas of Interest

49. Consumer complaint logs since the last examination.

50. Description of litigation, either filed or anticipated, associated with the bank's student lending activities. Include expected costs or other implications.

Transaction Testing

Examiners conduct transaction testing to verify compliance with the bank's policies and procedures; assess risk selection; determine accuracy of MIS; verify compliance with the applicable policies, laws, and regulations; and determine the accuracy of loan accounting and servicing.

51. Electronic files for each major student loan product that allow an examiner to select a sample to conduct the testing. The file should be provided in a format compatible with the National Credit Tool or an MS Excel worksheet that includes relevant loan information (e.g., account number, customer name, booking date, loan amount, payment information [current payment due, last payment date], loan term, interest rate, delinquency status, risk score, and repayment capacity measure). **Note:** Refer to appendix A, "Transaction Testing," of this booklet for areas and loans to be tested.

Appendix C: Uniform Retail Credit Classification and Account Management Policy Checklist

When using the Uniform Retail Credit Classification and Account Management Policy checklist, comment only in areas that apply to private student lending.

Uniform Retail Credit Classification and Account Management Policy (RCCP)		
Policy Applicability		
• Open- and closed-end credit extended to individuals for household, family, and other personal expenditures, including consumer loans, student loans, and credit cards. • Loans to individuals secured by their personal residences, including first mortgage, home equity, and home improvement loans.		
Note Regarding Minimum Policy Guidelines		
• The RCCP does not preclude examiners from classifying individual loans or entire portfolios regardless of delinquency status or criticizing account management practices that are deficient or improperly managed. If underwriting standards, risk management, or account management standards are weak and present unreasonable credit risk, deviation from the minimum classification guidelines outlined in the policy may be prudent. • Credit losses should be recognized when the bank becomes aware of the loss, but in no case should the charge-off exceed the time frames stated in the policy.		
	Reference	**Comments**
Substandard Classification 1. Does the bank consider open- and closed-end retail loans 90 cumulative days past due substandard? 2. When a bank does not hold the senior mortgage on home equity loans, does the bank consider the loans substandard if they are 90 days or more past due, even if the loan-to-value is 60 percent or less? **Note:** The policy states that properly secured residential real estate loans with loan-to-value ratios of 60 percent or less may not need to be classified based solely on delinquency. 3. For borrowers in bankruptcy and where the bank can clearly demonstrate that repayment is likely to occur, does the bank classify these loans as substandard until the borrower re-establishes his or her ability and willingness to repay for at least six months?		
Loss Classification 1. Are unsecured closed-end retail loans charged off in the month they become 120 cumulative days past due? 2. Are secured closed-end retail loans secured by other than real estate collateral charged off in the month they become 120 cumulative days past due? 3. If the answer to #2 is no, are these loans written down to the value of the collateral, less cost to sell, if repossession of collateral is assured and in process? 4. For open- and closed-end loans secured by residential real estate, is a current assessment of value made no later than when the account is 180 days past due? 5. For loans under #4, is any loan balance in excess of the value of the property, less cost to sell, charged off?		
Bankruptcy 1. Are loans in bankruptcy charged off within 60 days of receipt of notification of filing from the bankruptcy court or within the 120- or 180-day time frame (whichever is shorter)?		

	Reference	Comments
2. Are loans with collateral written down to the value of collateral, less cost to sell?		
3. When a loan's balance is not charged off, does the bank classify it as substandard until the borrower reestablishes the ability and willingness to repay for a period of at least six months?		
Fraudulent Loans		
• Are fraudulent loans classified loss and charged off within 90 days of discovery or within the 120- to 180-day time frame (whichever is shorter)?		
Deceased Accounts		
• Are loans of deceased persons classified loss and charged off when the loss is determined or within the 120- to 180-day time frame (whichever is shorter)?		
Other Considerations for Classification		
• Under what conditions would the bank not classify (substandard or loss) a loan in accordance with the policy? **Note:** The policy permits nonclassification if the bank can document that the loan is well-secured and in the process of collection, such that collection will occur regardless of delinquency status.		
Partial Payments		
1. Does the bank require that a payment be equivalent to 90 percent or greater of the contractual payment before counting the payment as a full payment?		
2. As an alternative, does the bank aggregate payments and give credit for any partial payments received?		
3. Are controls in place to prevent both methods above from being used simultaneously on the same credit?		
Re-Aging, Extensions, Deferrals, Renewals, and Rewrites		
1. Are these types of activities only permitted when the action is based on a renewed willingness and ability to repay the loan?		
2. Does documentation show that the bank communicated with the borrower, the borrower agreed to pay the loan in full, and the borrower has the ability to repay the loan?		
3. Does MIS separately identify the number of accounts and dollar amount that have been re-aged, extended, deferred, renewed, or rewritten, including the number of times such action has been taken?		
4. How does the bank monitor and track the volume and performance of loans that have been re-aged, extended, deferred, renewed, rewritten, or placed in a workout program? **Note:** Requirements 1 through 4 do not apply to customer-service-originated extensions or program extensions (such as holiday skip-a-pay). Examples of how the bank would determine and document the borrower's willingness and ability to repay could include such items as credit bureau score and data being obtained and reviewed, stated income being verified, and obtaining a "hardship" letter from the borrower.		

	Reference	Comments
Open-End Credit (Re-Aging) 1. Is a reasonable written policy in place and adhered to? 2. To be considered for re-aging, does the account exhibit the following: • Has the borrower demonstrated a renewed willingness and ability to repay the loan? • Has the account existed for at least nine months? • Has the borrower made at least three consecutive minimum monthly payments or the equivalent cumulative amount? • Does the bank prohibit the advancement of funds to make the minimum payment requirements? • Does the bank limit the number of re-ages to no more than once within any 12-month period? • Does the bank limit the frequency of re-ages to no more than twice within any five-year period? • For over-limit accounts that the bank re-ages, does the bank prohibit new credit from being extended until the balance falls below the pre-delinquency credit limit? 3. To be considered prudent, does the bank's workout loan program • require the receipt of at least three consecutive minimum monthly payments or the equivalent cumulative amount, as agreed to in the workout or debt management program, before re-aging an account that enters a workout program (internal or third party)? • limit re-ages to once in a five-year period? • have MIS that at a minimum tracks the principal reductions and charge-off history of loans in workout programs by type of program?		
Closed-End Credit (Standards, Controls, and MIS Required for Each Area) 1. Has the bank adopted and adhered to explicit standards that control the use of extensions, deferrals, renewals, and rewrites? 2. Do the standards include the following: • Has the borrower shown a renewed willingness and ability to repay the loan? • Do the standards limit the number and frequency of extensions, deferrals, renewals, and rewrites? • Are additional advances to finance unpaid interest and fees prohibited? 3. At a minimum, do MIS track the subsequent principal reductions and charge-off history of loans that have been granted an extension, deferral, renewal, or rewrite?		

Appendix D: Loss Forecasting Tool

Reliable forecasts of expected consumer charge-offs are critical for risk management, profitability, reserving, and capitalization. This appendix describes the three most common methods: roll rate models, historical averaging, and vintage-based forecasting. Some banks use combinations of all three methods for different consumer portfolios or forecasting purposes.

Roll Rates

Roll rate models are the most accurate short-term forecast technique. The name is derived from the practice of measuring the percentage of delinquent loans that migrate or "roll" from early delinquency to late-stage delinquency buckets, or to charge-off. The most common method is the delinquency roll rate model, in which dollars outstanding are stratified by delinquency status—typically, current, 30 to 59 days past due, 60 to 89 days past due, and so on through charge-off. The rates at which loans migrate or roll through delinquency levels are then used to project losses for the current portfolio. Figure 1 describes the mechanics of using roll rate analysis to track the migration of balances over a four-month period (120-day charge-off period).

Figure 1: Roll Rate Schematic

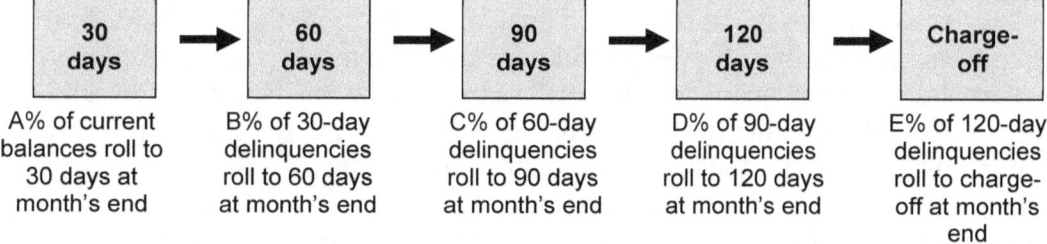

30 days	60 days	90 days	120 days	Charge-off
A% of current balances roll to 30 days at month's end	B% of 30-day delinquencies roll to 60 days at month's end	C% of 60-day delinquencies roll to 90 days at month's end	D% of 90-day delinquencies roll to 120 days at month's end	E% of 120-day delinquencies roll to charge-off at month's end

Step 1: Calculate roll rates

Step 1 is to calculate the roll rates. The following computation (figures 2 and 3) begins with the $725 million in loans that were current in June 2014. From June 2014 to July 2014, $27 million in loans migrated from current to 30 days delinquent, which equates to a roll rate of 3.73 percent ($27 ÷ $725). From July 2014 to August 2014, $10.6 million rolled to the next delinquency bucket, representing a 39.26 percent roll rate ($10.6 ÷ $27). Continuing along the shaded, stair-stepped boxes in the following table, loss rates increase in the latter stages of delinquency. To smooth out some fluctuations in the data, management often averages roll rates by quarter before making current portfolio forecasts, and compares quarterly roll rate results between quarters to analyze and adjust for seasonal effects.

The schematic and example in figures 2 and 3 are simplified depictions of dollar flow to illustrate the basic concept of roll rates. In reality, some balances cure (return to current), remain in the same delinquency bucket, or improve to a less severe delinquency status by the end of a period. For ease of calculation, roll rate analysis assumes all dollars at the end of a period flow from the previous period bucket.

Figure 2: Roll Rate Calculation by Outstanding Balance (in Millions)

Month (2014)	Current balance	30 days	Roll rate	60 days	Roll rate	90 days	Roll rate	120 days	Roll rate
June	$724.7	$26.1		$9.9		$6.7		$3.6	
July	$762.0	$27.0	3.73%	$10.9	41.77%	$7.1	71.27%	$4.7	70.36%
August	$788.6	$25.5	3.34%	$10.6	39.26%	$7.0	64.29%	$4.7	67.56%
September	$827.7	$29.4	3.73%	$12.1	47.82%	$7.9	74.88%	$5.5	78.74%
3rd-quarter averages			3.60%		42.95%		70.15%		72.22%
October	$844.6	$31.1	3.76%	$12.8	43.53%	$8.5	70.53%	$5.9	75.58%
November	$896.3	$26.7	3.16%	$12.4	40.03%	$8.2	64.52%	$5.9	69.49%
December	$987.3	$30.0	3.35%	$11.8	44.18%	$8.2	66.31%	$5.8	71.29%
4th-quarter averages			3.42%		42.58%		67.12%		72.12%
Loss factors			0.7%		20.61%		48.41%		72.12%

Step 2: Calculate loss factors by bucket

Step 2 is to calculate loss factors for each bucket. To calculate the loss factor from the "current" bucket, multiply all average roll rates from the most recent quarterly average. In this example, the fourth quarter average roll rates produce this factor: 3.42% x 42.58% x 67.12% x 72.12%, resulting in a 0.70 percent loss rate for loans in the current bucket. To determine the loss rate for the 30-day accounts, multiply the most recent quarterly averages for the 60-, 90-, and 120-day buckets, resulting in a loss factor of 20.61 percent. Applying the same method results in a loss factor of 48.41 percent for the 60-day bucket and 72.12 percent for the 90-day bucket.

Step 3: Apply loss factors to the current portfolio

Figure 3: Loss Forecast Using Roll Rates

December 31, 2014	Outstandings (in millions)	Loss factor	Loss forecast (in millions)
Current days	$987.4	0.7%	$6.9
30	$30.2	20.61%	$6.2
60	$11.8	48.41%	$5.7
90	$8.2	72.12%	$5.9
120	$5.9	100%	$5.9
Totals	$1,043.5	2.93%	$30.6

Step 3 is to forecast losses for the existing portfolio by applying the loss factors for each bucket (developed in step 2) to the current portfolio. In this example, the portfolio's expected loss rate over the next four months is 2.93 percent.

The major advantage of roll rate analysis is its relative simplicity and considerable accuracy out to nine months. Portfolios are often segmented by product, customer type, or other relevant groupings to increase precision and accuracy. Collection managers use roll rate reports extensively to anticipate workload and staffing needs and to assess and adjust collection strategies.

The main limitation of roll rates is that the predictive power of delinquency roll rate declines after nine months. The delinquency focus causes forecasts to lag underlying changes in portfolio quality, especially in the relatively large current bucket. Portfolio quality changes occur because of such factors as underwriting and cutoff score adjustments, product mix changes, and shifts in economic conditions. Roll rate analysis may underestimate loss exposure when these factors cause portfolio quality to weaken. Finally, roll rate methodology assumes loans migrate through an orderly succession of delinquency stages before charge-off. In actuality, customers often migrate to charge-off status after sporadic payments or rush to that status by declaring bankruptcy.

Historical

Historical averaging is a rudimentary method for forecasting loss rates. Management tracks historical charge-offs, adjusts for recent loss experience trends, and adds some qualitative recognition of current economic conditions or changes in portfolio mix. This method is highly judgmental and is used primarily by less sophisticated banks, or for stable, conservatively underwritten products. The most common of these products are residential mortgages when the collateral protection is conservative or the loans carry some sort of third-party guaranty or insurance.

The method is sometimes used for allowance purposes and monitoring general product or portfolio trends. The advantage is simplicity, and data needs are modest. Results can be reasonably accurate as long as underwriting standards remain relatively constant and economic or competitive conditions do not change markedly. The major limitation is that forecasts will lag behind underlying changes in portfolio quality if competitive or economic conditions change. The judgmental nature of the process introduces potential bias by allowing forecasters to rely on longer run averages when conditions deteriorate and short-run trends at the earliest signs of recovery, either of which results in lower loss estimates. In addition, the method does not provide meaningful information on the effects of changes in product or customer mix, and it is difficult to apply any but the most basic stress tests.

Vintage

Vintage-based forecasting tracks delinquency and loss curves by time on books as different vintages or marketing campaign seasons. The patterns or curves are predictive for future vintages, if adjustments are made for changes in underwriting criteria, altered cutoffs, and economic conditions. The advantage of vintage-based forecasting is that its accuracy is usually better than roll rate forecasts for charge-offs beyond a one-year horizon, if the need for adjustments is readily observed. Management should adjust the future loss expectations when new vintages are observed to deviate markedly from past curves and trajectories, or if economic and market conditions change. The disadvantages of vintage-based forecasting are that it is more subjective and less accurate than roll rates for short-term forecasting and that it relies on the assumption that new vintages will perform similarly to older vintages.

Appendix E: Glossary

Note: Sources include the U.S. Department of Education, the *Common Manual*, and industry websites, including FinAid.

Academic year: The period during which school is in session, consisting of at least 30 weeks of instructional time. The academic year typically runs from approximately the beginning of September through the end of May at most colleges and universities.

Allowance for loan and lease losses (ALLL): A valuation reserve that represents an estimate of uncollectible amounts (probable and incurred losses) that is used to reduce the book value of loans and leases to the amount that is expected to be collected. The allowance is established and maintained by charges against the bank's operating income, that is, the provision expense.

Amortization: The process of gradually repaying a loan over a period of time through periodic installments of principal and interest.

Award letter: An official document issued by a school's financial aid office that lists all of the financial aid awarded to the student.

Award year: The academic year for which financial aid is requested (or received). The period from July 1 of a given calendar year through June 30 of the following calendar year.

Bankruptcy: Judicial action to stay the normal collection of debts against the petitioner and cause those debts deemed to be satisfied at the direction of the court. Bankruptcies are classified under the U.S. Code by "chapters," which refer to parts of the U.S. Bankruptcy Code.

Campus-based programs: The Federal Perkins Loan, Federal Work-Study, and Federal Supplemental Educational Opportunity Grant programs. These programs and their related funds are administered directly by a school's financial aid office. In return, the school is allowed to retain a percentage of each program's funds for its administrative costs. Awards are made from a fixed pool of money.

Cancellation: Loan cancellation ends the obligation to repay the debt and typically involves the discharge or forgiveness of the loan balance (including any accrued but unpaid interest).

Capitalization: The practice of adding unpaid interest charges to the principal balance of a loan. Interest is then charged on the new balance, including both the unpaid principal and the accrued interest.

Cohort default rate (CDR): The percentage of borrowers in the cohort who default on certain loans made under federal student loan programs before the end of the second fiscal year after the fiscal year in which they entered repayment on their loans. The Education

Department releases information on CDRs annually. For more information on the CDR and how it is calculated, refer to the Education Department's website.

Collection agency: A company often hired by the lender or guarantee agency to recover defaulted loans.

Consolidation loan: Also called loan consolidation, a consolidation loan combines several student loans into one larger loan from a single lender. The consolidation loan is like a refinance and is used to pay off the balances on the other loans.

Cosigner: Any person who assumes personal liability, in any capacity, for the obligation of a borrower without receiving goods, services, or money in return for the obligation. The cosigner is equally and severally liable and is expected to make payments on the primary borrower's debt should that person default.

Cost of attendance: An estimate of the student's educational expenses for the period of enrollment.

Credit history: A credit history is a record of all events connected with payment of a set of debts, such as on-time payments, late payments, nonpayment, default, liens, and bankruptcy discharge. A credit history can include both current and previous credit accounts and their balances, employment and personal information, and history of past credit problems.

Credit scoring: A statistical method for predicting the creditworthiness of applicants and existing customers.

Default: A loan is in default when the borrower fails to pay several regular installments on time or otherwise fails to meet the terms and conditions of the loan. A borrower who is 120 days late on a private student loan or 270 days late on a federal education loan is considered to be in default.

Default fee: Synonymous with guarantee fee. A guarantee is an agreement to purchase title to a loan if the borrower defaults on his or her obligation to repay the debt.

Deferment: Occurs when a borrower is allowed to postpone repaying the loan.

Delinquent: A period that begins on the day after the due date of a payment when the borrower fails to make a full payment.

Dependency status: A measure of the degree to which a student has access to his or her parents' financial resources.

Direct loans: The William D. Ford Federal Direct Loan Program (Direct Loan Program) is a federal program in which the school becomes the lending agency and manages the funds directly, with the federal government providing the loan funds. The terms for direct loans are the same as for loans issued under the Stafford Loan program.

Direct Parental Loans for Undergraduate Students (Direct PLUS Loans): A federal student loan available to graduate or professional degree students and parents of dependent undergraduate students to help pay education expenses. Parents may borrow up to the full cost of their children's education, minus the amount of any other financial aid received. Direct PLUS Loans may be used to pay the expected family contribution. There is a minimal credit check required for the Direct PLUS loan.

Disbursement: The transfer of loan proceeds by individual check, master check, or electronic funds transfer by a lender to a borrower, a school, or an escrow agent.

Discharge: The release of a borrower or any cosigner from all or a portion of his or her loan obligation.

Disclosure statement: Provides the borrower with information about the actual cost of the loan, including the interest rate, origination, insurance, loan fees, and any other types of finance charges. Lenders are required to provide the borrower with a disclosure statement before issuing a loan.

Electronic data exchange: Program used by participating schools to receive Student Aid Reports electronically from the federal processor. At some schools, this program allows students to file their FAFSA electronically.

Enrollment status: An indication of whether a student is attending school full time or part time.

Entitlement: Entitlement programs award money to all qualified applicants. The Pell Grant is an example of such a program. The Individuals With Disabilities Education Act Federal Special Education Entitlement Grant is another example.

Expanded lending option: Under this option, some schools can offer higher annual and cumulative loan limits to students receiving a Perkins Loan. The expanded lending option is restricted to schools with a Perkins Loan default rate of 15 percent or less.

Expected family contribution (EFC): The amount a student and the student's spouse or family are expected to pay toward the student's cost of attendance.

Federal Family Education Loan Program (FFELP): A discontinued student loan program authorized by Title IV, part B, of the HEA, as amended. FFELP included subsidized and unsubsidized Stafford, Direct PLUS, and consolidation loans. These loans were funded by lenders, guaranteed by guarantors, and reinsured by the Education Department.

Federal methodology: The need analysis formula used to determine the EFC. The federal methodology takes into account the family size, the number of family members in college, taxable and nontaxable income, and assets. Unlike most institutional methodologies, the federal methodology does not consider the net value of the family residence.

Financial aid: Money provided to the student and the family to help them pay for the student's education, which is conditioned on the student's attendance at an educational institution. Major forms of financial aid include gift aid (grants and scholarships) and self-help aid (loans and work).

Financial Aid Administrator: A staff member at an eligible school who administers financial aid programs.

Financial Aid Office: The college or university office that is responsible for determining financial need and awarding financial aid.

Financial aid package: The total amount of financial aid that a school awards a student. Federal and nonfederal aid such as loans, grants, or work-study are combined into a "package" to help meet the student's cost of attendance. Using available resources to give each student the best possible aid package is one of the major responsibilities of a school's financial aid administrator.

Financial aid transcript: An official record of the federal financial aid that a student received at schools the student previously attended. The record is used to assess the amount of federal financial aid the student has received and to prevent the award of federal funds for which the student or the parent of a dependent student is not eligible. The record may be obtained from the NSLDS or may be a paper report received from the previous schools.

Forbearance: A period of time during which the borrower is permitted to temporarily cease making payments or reduce the amount of the payments for reasons including certain types of financial hardships. The borrower is liable for the interest that accrues on the loan during the forbearance period.

Forgiveness: Loan forgiveness releases the borrower from his or her obligation to repay the loan, usually due to circumstances within the borrower's control. For student loans, the most common loan forgiveness programs cancel all or part of the debt for working in a particular field or performing military or volunteer service. Loan forgiveness for working in a particular occupation is tax-free; other types of loan forgiveness may result in a tax liability. There are two main types of loan forgiveness: up-front and back-end. Up-front loan forgiveness cancels a portion of the debt for each year of service. Back-end loan forgiveness cancels any remaining debt after a specified number of years of service. Forgiveness is a type of loan cancellation.

Free Application for Federal Student Aid (FAFSA): The form the student must complete to apply for federal Title IV financial assistance, including Stafford Loans. The student must include financial information about the student's household so that the EFC can be calculated.

Garnishment: The practice of withholding a portion of a defaulted borrower's wages to repay his or her loan, without consent.

Grace period: A time period after graduation during which the borrower is not required to begin repaying his or her student loans. The grace period may also apply if the borrower leaves school for a reason other than graduation or drops below half-time enrollment. Depending on the type of loan, a borrower has a grace period of six months (Stafford Loans and private student loans) or nine months (Perkins Loans) before the borrower must start making payments. PLUS Loans do not have a grace period. CNBE Policy Guidance 2010-2 (REV), "Policy Interpretation: OCC Bulletin 2000-20—Application to Private Student Lending," allows a grace period of six months for private student loans, with an additional six-month extended grace period if the borrower can document financial hardship.

Graduated repayment schedule: A repayment schedule under which the borrower pays lower initial monthly payments that gradually increase (usually in two or more increments) during the course of the repayment period. For federal student loans, the graduated repayment schedule cannot exceed 10 years (or 25 years for borrowers eligible for an extended repayment schedule), excluding in-school, grace, deferment, and forbearance periods.

Grant: A type of financial aid based on financial need that the student does not have to repay.

Guarantee: A guarantee is an agreement to purchase title to a loan if the borrower defaults on his or her obligation to repay the debt.

Guarantee agency or guarantor: State agencies responsible for approving student loans and insuring them against default. Guarantee agencies also oversee the student loan process and enforce federal and state rules regarding student loans.

Guarantee fee: A small percentage of the loan that is paid to the guarantee agency to insure the loan against default. The insurance fee is usually 1 percent of the loan amount. Also known as a default fee.

Half time: An enrollment status under which a student in an undergraduate program is carrying an academic workload that includes at least half of the academic workload of the required minimum full-time enrollment standard for that program.

Income-Based Repayment Plan: A repayment plan available to a borrower who has a partial financial hardship or is paying a permanent-standard payment amount after qualifying for such a hardship. If a lender determines that a borrower has a partial hardship, the borrower's monthly payment amount on eligible loans is limited to 15 percent of the amount by which the borrower's annual adjusted gross income exceeds 150 percent of the U.S. Department of Health and Human Services' poverty guideline for the borrower's family size. The Education Department repays the outstanding balance and accrued interest on eligible FFELP and direct loans after 25 years and a combination of 300 months covered by qualifying payments or economic hardship deferments, beginning no earlier than July 1, 2009.

Income-Contingent Repayment Plan: A repayment schedule for some Direct Loan Program loans under which the borrower's monthly payment amount is adjusted annually, based on the total amount of the borrower's direct loans, the borrower's family size, and the adjusted gross income reported on the borrower's most recent income tax return. In the case of a married borrower who files a joint income tax return, the adjusted gross income includes the spouse's income.

Income-Sensitive Repayment Plan: A repayment schedule for some FFELP loans under which the borrower's monthly payment amount is adjusted annually, based solely on the borrower's expected total monthly gross income received from employment and other sources during the course of the repayment period.

Independent student: An independent student is at least 24 years old as of January 1 of the academic year, is married, is a graduate or professional student, has a legal dependent other than a spouse, is a veteran of the U.S. Armed Forces, or is an orphan or ward of the court (or was a ward of the court until age 18). A parent refusing to provide support for his or her child's education is not sufficient for the child to be declared independent.

Lender subsidies: A set of arrangements established to encourage lenders to make federally guaranteed education loans. These arrangements include a federal guarantee against borrower default, special allowance payments, and lender-paid origination fees.

LIBOR: The LIBOR, or London Interbank Offered Rate, is a variable rate index that typically reflects the rates that financial institutions charge one another for short-term loans.

Loan servicer: A loan servicer is a business that collects payments on a loan and performs other administrative tasks associated with maintaining a loan portfolio.

National credit bureau: A credit reporting agency with a service area encompassing more than a single region of the country.

National Student Loan Data System (NSLDS): A database comprising information from guarantors, schools, lenders, and the Education Department on Title IV aid received by students.

Out-of-pocket cost: Out-of-pocket cost is the difference between the cost of attendance and the grants, scholarships, and other gift aid in the need-based financial aid package. It reflects the bottom line cost to the family, that is, the amount the family will need to pay out of current and future resources, such as savings, income, and loans. Some nonprofit colleges that have adopted no-loans financial aid policies have lower out-of-pocket costs than many public colleges. Generally, families should evaluate college financial aid award letters using out-of-pocket cost.

Out-of-state student: A student who has not met the legal residency requirements for the state and is often charged a higher tuition rate at public colleges and universities in the state than legal residents.

Overawards: A student who receives federal support may not receive awards totaling more than $400 in excess of his or her financial need.

Packaging: The process of assembling a financial aid package.

Parent contribution: An estimate of the portion of educational expenses that the federal government believes parents can afford. It is based on the parents' income, the number of parents earning income, assets, family size, the number of family members currently attending a university or college, and other relevant factors. Students who qualify as independent are not expected to have a parent contribution.

Participating school: An eligible school that meets the standards for participation in Title IV programs, has a current program participation agreement with the Education Department, and is eligible to receive funds under these programs.

Pell Grant: A federal grant that provides up to $5,815 (in 2016–2017) based on the student's financial need.

Perkins Loan: Formerly the National Direct Student Loan Program, the Perkins Loan allows students to borrow up to $3,000 per year (up to a five-year maximum) for undergraduate school and $5,000 per year for graduate school (up to a six-year maximum). The Perkins Loan has one of the lowest interest rates and is awarded by the school's financial aid administrator to students with exceptional financial need. The student must have applied for a Pell Grant to be eligible. The interest on the Perkins Loan is subsidized while the student is in school.

Poverty line: The poverty guidelines, often referred to as the poverty line, are published annually by the U.S. Department of Health and Human Services. The guidelines are a simplification of the poverty thresholds published annually by the U.S. Census Bureau. The poverty line is more often used in federal student aid, such as the Income-Based Repayment and Income-Contingent Repayment plans, as well as the economic hardship deferment.

Preferred lender arrangement: An arrangement or agreement between a lender and a school or an institution-affiliated organization under which the lender provides or otherwise issues private education loans to students attending the school (or to the students' families) and under which the school or institution-affiliated organization recommends, promotes, or endorses the lender's education loan products.

Prime lending rate: The prime lending rate is the interest rate offered by lenders to their best credit customers.

Private student loans: Education loan programs without a guarantee from the federal government.

Professional degree: A degree that signifies both completion of the academic requirements for beginning practice in a given profession and a level of professional skill beyond that normally required for a bachelor's degree. Professional licensure is also generally required. Examples of a professional degree include pharmacy (Pharm. D.), law (LLB or JD), and medicine (MD).

Rehabilitation (of a defaulted loan): A process by which a borrower may bring a FFELP loan out of default by adhering to specified repayment requirements.

Reinstatement (of borrower Title IV eligibility): A process by which a borrower with a defaulted FFELP loan may regain eligibility for Title IV aid by adhering to strict repayment requirements

Repayment period: The period during which payments of principal and interest are required. The repayment period follows any applicable in-school or grace period.

Satisfactory academic progress: The qualitative (grade point average) and quantitative (time limit) measures of a student's progress toward completing a program of study. To maintain eligibility for Title IV aid, the student must show adequate progress. A school must establish policies regarding satisfactory academic progress and must check the progress of Title IV aid recipients at least once each academic year, or at the end of each payment period if the educational program is either one academic year in length or shorter than an academic year.

Scholarship: A form of financial aid given to undergraduate students to help pay for their education. Most scholarships are restricted to paying all or part of tuition expenses, though some scholarships also cover room and board. Scholarships are a form of gift aid and do not have to be repaid. Many scholarships are restricted to students in specific courses of study or with academic, athletic, or artistic talent.

Skip tracing: Diligent efforts to locate a borrower's telephone number or address when such information is unknown.

Special allowance payments: Special allowance payments were established for FFELP to ensure that education lenders received a market rate of return on federal education loans. Whenever the borrower interest rate on the federal education loans fell below market rates, the Education Department would make special allowance payments to the lenders based on the difference between the interest rates.

Stafford Loans: Federal student loans that come in two forms, subsidized and unsubsidized. Subsidized loans are based on need, unsubsidized loans are not. The interest on a Subsidized Stafford Loan is paid by the federal government while the student is in school and during a six-month grace period. The Subsidized Stafford Loan was formerly known as the Guaranteed Student Loan.

Student Aid Report: The paper output record provided to the student by the Education Department's Central Processing System that includes information provided by the student on the FAFSA. The report also contains the student's EFC and the results of federal database matches. The electronic version that is sent to schools is called an Institutional Student Information Record.

Subrogation: A transfer in the ownership of a defaulted FFELP loan from a guarantor to the Education Department. Loans to be subrogated must meet criteria established and revised annually by the department.

Subsidized loan: A loan eligible for interest benefits paid by the federal government. The federal government pays the interest that accrues on subsidized loans during the student's in-school, authorized deferment, and (if applicable) post-deferment grace periods, if the loan meets certain eligibility requirements.

Treasury offset: An interception by the U.S. Department of the Treasury or a state agency of any payment of applicable federal funds (tax refunds, Social Security benefits, federal retirement benefits, etc.) or state funds otherwise due a borrower who has defaulted on a FFELP loan.

Troubled debt restructuring (TDR): A restructuring in which a bank, for economic or other reasons related to a borrower's financial difficulties, grants a concession to the borrower that it would not otherwise consider. This includes a modification of the loan terms, such as a reduction of the stated interest rate, principal, or accrued interest or an extension of the maturity date at a stated interest rate lower than the current market rate for new debt with similar risk.

U.S. Department of Education: The federal government agency that administers several federal student financial aid programs, including the Federal Pell Grant, the Federal Work-Study Program, the Federal Perkins Loans, the Federal Stafford Loans, and the Federal PLUS Loans.

William D. Ford Federal Direct Loan Program (Direct Loan Program): A student loan program authorized in 1992 by Title IV, part D, of the HEA, as amended. The Direct Loan program offers four components: Direct Subsidized Stafford Loans, Direct Unsubsidized Stafford Loans, Direct PLUS Loans, and Direct Consolidation Loans. The Direct Loan program is similar to the discontinued FFELP, except that loans are made by the Education Department rather than by private lending institutions.

Appendix F: Abbreviations

ALLL	allowance for loan and lease losses
CDR	cohort default rate
CFPB	Consumer Financial Protection Bureau
CNBE	Chief National Bank Examiner
COA	cost of attendance
ECOA	Equal Credit Opportunity Act
EFC	expected family contribution
EFTA	Electronic Fund Transfer Act
EIC	examiner-in-charge
FAFSA	Free Application for Federal Student Aid
FCRA	Fair Credit Reporting Act
FDCPA	Fair Debt Collection Practices Act
FFELP	Federal Family Education Loan Program
FFIEC	Federal Financial Institutions Examination Council
FSA	federal savings association
GAAP	generally accepted accounting principles
GLBA	Gramm–Leach–Bliley Act
HCERA	Health Care and Education Rehabilitation Act
HEA	Higher Education Act
ICQ	internal control questionnaire
LIBOR	London Interbank Offered Rate
MIS	management information systems

MLA	Military Lending Act
NSLDS–SSCR	National Student Loan Data System–Student Status Confirmation Report
OCC	Office of the Comptroller of the Currency
RCCP	Retail Credit Classification and Account Management Policy
ROE	report of examination
SCRA	Servicemembers Civil Relief Act
SSAE	Statement on Standards for Attestation Engagements
TDR	troubled debt restructuring
TILA	Truth in Lending Act
UDAAP	Unfair, Deceptive or Abusive Acts or Practices
UDAP	Unfair or Deceptive Acts or Practices

References

Laws

12 USC 24, "Corporate Powers of Associations" (national banks)
12 USC 161, "Reports to Comptroller of the Currency" (national banks)
12 USC 484, "Limitation on Visitorial Powers" (national banks)
12 USC 1461 et seq., "Home Owners' Loan Act" (federal savings associations)
15 USC 45, "Unfair Methods of Competition Unlawful"
15 USC 1601, et seq., "Truth in Lending Act"
15 USC 1681, et seq., "Fair Credit Reporting Act"
15 USC 1691, et seq., "Equal Credit Opportunity Act"
15 USC 1692, et seq., "Fair Debt Collection Practices Act"
15 USC 6801, et seq., "Gramm–Leach–Bliley Act"
20 USC 1001 et seq., "Higher Education Act," Pub. L. No. 89-329, Title IV, part D
50 USC 3901 et seq., "Servicemembers Civil Relief Act"
"Health Care and Education Reconciliation Act," Pub. L. No. 111-152, Title II, section 2201

Regulations

12 CFR 3, subpart C (12 CFR 3.20–3.22), "Definition of Capital"
12 CFR 3, subpart D (12 CFR 3.30–3.63), "Risk-Weighted Assets–Standardized Approach"
12 CFR 3, subpart E (12 CFR 3.100–3.173), "Risk-Weighted Assets–Internal Ratings-Based and Advanced Measurement Approaches"
12 CFR 7, "Bank Activities and Operations"
12 CFR 21.11, "Suspicious Activity Reports"
12 CFR 30, "Safety and Soundness Standards"
12 CFR 128, "Nondiscrimination Requirements" (federal savings associations)
12 CFR 160, "Lending and Investment" (federal savings associations)
12 CFR 162, "Regulatory Reporting Standards" (federal savings associations)
12 CFR 163.176, "Interest-Rate-Risk-Management Procedures" (federal savings associations)

Comptroller's Handbook

Examination Process
"Bank Supervision Process"
"Community Bank Supervision"
"Federal Branches and Agencies Supervision"
"Large Bank Supervision"
"Sampling Methodologies"

Safety and Soundness, Asset Quality
"Allowance for Loan and Lease Losses"
"Loan Portfolio Management"

"Rating Credit Risk"

Safety and Soundness, Liquidity
"Asset Securitization"

Safety and Soundness, Management
"Internal and External Audits"
"Internal Control"

Consumer Compliance
"Fair Credit Reporting"
"Fair Lending"
"Other Consumer Protection Laws and Regulations"
"Privacy of Consumer Financial Information"
"Servicemembers Civil Relief Act"
"Truth in Lending Act"

OCC Issuances

Advisory Letter 2000-7, "Abusive Lending Practices" (July 25, 2000)
Advisory Letter 2002-3, "Guidance on Unfair or Deceptive Acts or Practices" (March 22, 2002)
Advisory Letter 2003-2, "Guidelines for National Banks to Guard Against Predatory and Abusive Lending Practices" (February 21, 2003)
CNBE Policy Guidance 2010-2 (REV), "Policy Interpretation: OCC Bulletin 2000-20— Application to Private Student Lending" (May 9, 2016)
OCC Bulletin 1997-24, "Credit Scoring Models: Examination Guidance" (May 20, 1997) (not applicable to FSAs)
OCC Bulletin 1999-10, "Subprime Lending Activities" (March 5, 1999)
OCC Bulletin 1999-15, "Subprime Lending: Risks and Rewards" (April 5, 1999) (not applicable to FSAs)
OCC Bulletin 2000-3, "Consumer Credit Reporting Practices: FFIEC Advisory Letter" (February 16, 2000)
OCC Bulletin 2000-20, "Uniform Retail Credit Classification and Account Management Policy: Policy Implementation" (June 20, 2000)
OCC Bulletin 2001-6, "Subprime Lending: Expanded Guidance for Subprime Lending Programs" (January 31, 2001)
OCC Bulletin 2001-37, "Policy Statement on Allowance for Loan and Lease Losses Methodologies and Documentation for Banks and Savings Institutions: ALLL Methodologies and Documentation" (July 20, 2001)
OCC Bulletin 2003-01, "Credit Card Lending: Account Management and Loss Allowance Guidance" (January 8, 2003)
OCC Bulletin 2004-20, "Risk Management of New, Expanded, or Modified Bank Products and Services: Risk Management Process" (May 10, 2004) (national banks; for FSAs, refer to the *OTS Examination Handbook*, section 760)

OCC Bulletin 2006-47, "Allowance for Loan and Lease Losses (ALLL): Guidance and Frequently Asked Questions (FAQ) on the ALLL" (December 13, 2006)

OCC Bulletin 2011-12, "Supervisory Guidance on Model Risk Management" (April 4, 2011)

OCC Bulletin 2011-16, "Servicemembers Civil Relief Act: Revised Examination Procedures" (May 3, 2011)

OCC Bulletin 2012-10, "Troubled Debt Restructurings: Supervisory Guidance on Accounting and Reporting Requirements" (April 5, 2012)

OCC Bulletin 2013-29, "Third-Party Relationships: Risk Management Guidance" (October 20, 2013)

OCC Bulletin 2014-42, "Interagency Guidance Regarding Unfair or Deceptive Credit Practices" (August 22, 2014)

OCC Bulletin 2015-7, "Interagency Guidance on Private Student Loans With Graduated Repayment Terms at Origination" (January 29, 2015)